THE SWAZI
A South African Kingdom

By

HILDA KUPER
University of California

HOLT, RINEHART AND WINSTON

NEW YORK   CHICAGO   SAN FRANCISCO   TORONTO   LONDON

I should like to acknowledge the assistance given me by the African Studies Center of the University of California and its Director, Dr. James S. Coleman, through a grant for the preparation of the manuscript. I also want to thank the International African Institute for its permission to use extensively material published in my previous books, *An African Aristocracy* and *The Swazi*.

CASE STUDIES IN
CULTURAL ANTHROPOLOGY

GENERAL EDITORS

George and Louise Spindler

STANFORD UNIVERSITY

THE SWAZI

A South African Kingdom

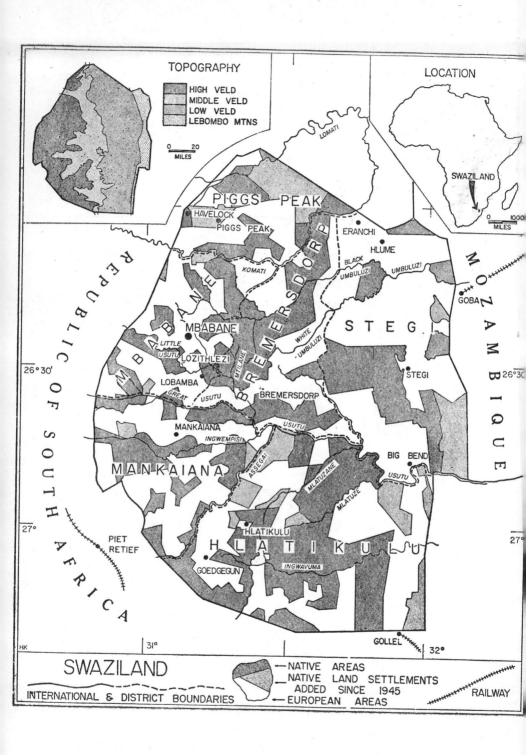

TOPOGRAPHY

HIGH VELD
MIDDLE VELD
LOW VELD
LEBOMBO MTNS

0   20
MILES

LOCATION

SWAZILAND

0   1000
MILES

LOMATI

PIGGS PEAK

HAVELOCK
PIGGS PEAK

ERANCHI

HLUME

BLACK
UMBULUZI   UMBULUZI

KOMATI

GOBA

R E P U B L I C

B R E M E R S D O R P

M B A B A N E

MBABANE

WHITE
UMBULUZI

S T E G I

LITTLE
USUTU
LOZITHLEZI

M T L A N E

26°30'

26°30

LOBAMBA

GREAT   USUTU

BREMERSDORP

STEGI

O F   S O U T H

MANKAIANA

USUTU

INGWEMPISI

BIG BEND

M A N K A I A N A

ASSEGAI

USUTU

MLATUZANE

MLATUZE

27°

27°

A F R I C A

PIET
RETIEF

HLATIKULU

H L A T I K U L U

GOEDGEGUN

INGWAVUMA

M O Z A M B I Q U E

HK

31°

GOLLEL

32°

SWAZILAND

NATIVE   AREAS
NATIVE   LAND   SETTLEMENTS
              ADDED   SINCE   1945
EUROPEAN   AREAS

INTERNATIONAL & DISTRICT BOUNDARIES

RAILWAY

The (late) Queen Mother, Lomawa, in leopard-skin cloak, at the ceremony of kingship.

A senior age group in full regalia.

Carrying the framework of a hut to a new site.

Mpundla Maziya, a chief of the old order.

The reluctant bride.

Foreword

About the Series

These case studies in cultural anthropology are designed to bring to students in beginning and intermediate courses in the social sciences insights into the richness and complexty of human life as it is lived in different ways and in different places. They are written by men and women who have lived in the societies they write about and who are professionally trained as observers and interpreters of human behavior. The authors are also teachers, and in writing their books they have kept the students who will read them foremost in their minds. It is our belief that when an understanding of ways of life very different from one's own is gained, abstractions and generalizations about social structure, cultural values, subsistence techniques, and other universal categories of human social behavior become meaningful.

About the Author

Hilda Kuper is Research Fellow of the African Studies Center, University of California, Los Angeles. She was born in Rhodesia and studied anthropology in Johannesburg and London, where she obtained her doctorate at the London School of Economics. She spent two years doing field research in Swaziland as a Fellow of the International African Institute. She has taught anthropology at Witwatersrand University, Johannesburg, and at the University of Natal, Durban. She has also held a senior Simon Research Fellowship at the University of Manchester, England, and has lectured in England and America. She has published much on the Swazi, including her well-known book, *An African Aristocracy*. Her play, "A Witch in My Heart," has been translated into Zulu and published by Shooter and Shooter.

About the Book

This book describes a way of life that is strange to the Western eye and mind. Swazi society is highly structured, with a centralized state and a dual monarchy—the king and the queen mother—that is always in a delicate state of balance. The interlocking of clans and lineages, the functions and meaning of the homestead with its patriarchal headman, his wives, and other dependents, and the relations of these units with the royal lineage and household are all interrelated into a complex system that Dr. Kuper makes very clear to the reader. The full meaning of the Swazi way of life becomes most dramatically apparent in the description of religion, magic, sorcery, and ceremonial. We see how incongruent Western and Swazi con-

▼

cepts are, and come to understand the difficulties the Swazi encounter in making a smooth adjustment to the modern Western way of life.

The analysis developed by Dr. Kuper is functional, in keeping with her English training, but history is not left out. We see how the clans were welded into a centralized state by the conquering Nguni aristocracy and then how this state lost much of its power to the Boers and British. And in the last chapter Dr. Kuper describes how the impact of Western industrialization threatens the basis of traditional Swazi soicety. It is clear that the result of the economic and social transformation that is taking place will be a way of life rather different from ours, for the Swazi past extends into the Swazi future.

GEORGE AND LOUISE SPINDLER
General Editors

Stanford, California
1963

Contents

To Jenny and Mary

Introduction

THE SWAZI are part of the millions of Bantu-speaking peoples of Africa who migrated at different times from places farther north and eventually arrived in the southeastern region between the Drakensberg Mountains and the Indian Ocean.* From their homelands they brought cattle and seed for cultivation, and handmade products of iron, wood, skin, and clay. They did not use their cattle for transport, and, being their own beasts of burden, they probably traveled light. But they carried with them the heritage of all immigrants—the knowledge, memories, and experiences of the past from societies they had left behind. With this, they were able to shape their lives anew, adapting as they forgot.

The country they traversed was inhabited by peoples—hunters and pastoral nomads—whose ways of life were different from their own, and there was also infiltration from non-African outsiders along the eastern seaboard, where they settled. Long before the arrival of white settlers in the southeast, there was contact, to the point of intermarriage, between different groups. The modern Swazi, a handsome people, are predominantly Negroid in appearance, but with skin color ranging from dark brown to honey gold; occasional individuals have profiles reminiscent of friezes from ancient Egypt and others show Bushmanoid features. Distinct from physical mingling there occurred cultural diffusion and borrowing, and social adjustments, which may account for some of the striking similarities in both culture (material goods and the less tangible aspects of social beliefs and behavior) and social structure (ordered systems of relationship), found in areas far apart on the vast African continent.

Traditional Africa presents several models of political systems, ranging from large-scale states and highly centralized chiefdoms to small local commu-

---

* _Bantu_, literally "People," is a linguistic label derived from the root _ntu_, "person," and the plural prefix _ba_. There are over 400 Bantu languages and many dialects, but their structure is sufficiently characteristic and distinctive to postulate a common origin.

1

nities, knit primarily by kinship and without defined political leadership. In the process of historical growth, the Swazi developed their particular system, a dual monarchy that was unique in some respects but which fits into the general category of centralized chiefdoms. At the head was a hereditary king, titled by his people *Ingwenyama* (Lion), and a queen mother, *Indlovukati* (Lady Elephant).

Beginning in the nineteenth century, boundaries drawn by white colonial powers cut through existing African political units. Swazi tribesmen found themselves dispersed in territories controlled by British, Boer (Afrikaner), and Portuguese. At present, the claim to Swazi identity remains based on allegiance to the two traditional rulers, but Swazi living in the Republic (formerly the Union) of South Africa and in the Portuguese province of Lourenço Marques fall outside their effective control. This book is limited to the way of life of those Swazi whose homes are in the small British High Commission Territory of Swaziland, where the *Ingwenyama* is recognized as the paramount chief in the new bureaucracy, and the *Indlovukati* is titled queen mother.

Swaziland, a lovely country of 6704 square miles—roughly the size of Hawaii—offers the challenge of considerable regional variation. In the west are rugged highlands where grass is short and sour, trees grow mainly in deep ravines, and the weather is cold and exhilarating. The mountains slope into the undulating plains of the more fertile and warmer midlands, which, in turn, gradually give place to bush country where cattle thrive throughout the year on green foliage. Between the lowlands and the eastern seaboard, the windswept Lebombo Range forms the fourth topographical region.

Of great cultural importance to the Swazi is the abundant supply of water. Rain comes with the beginning of spring, in August or September, and falls in heavy showers, saturating the land and filling four large rivers and many tributaries, until the end of summer, in January or February. Throughout southern Africa, the Swazi queen mother is famed for her rain medicine. Her people do not consider floods and droughts acts of God or nature, but signs of royal displeasure or punishment from royal ancestral spirits. In more arid areas it is safer for the rulers to employ others as rainmakers. In Swaziland rain supports the traditional monarchy.

Its temperate climate, fertile soil, and potential wealth have made Swaziland an area of white settlement. In 1946 the population was approximately 184,750, of whom 181,000 were Africans, 3000 Europeans ("whites"), and 750 EurAfricans, ("coloreds," people of "mixed" descent). The whites own roughly half the territory, and the majority of Swazi are concentrated in scattered reservations, called "Native Areas" or "Swazi Areas." Swaziland illustrates graphically the point that geographical conditions and natural resources are subservient to social controls. The territory presents an economic patchwork, reflecting largely a pattern of land distribution between whites and non-whites, irrespective of the four major topographical belts into which the country falls. All major advances in mining, agriculture, industry, and commerce are concentrated in "European areas." Like most of modern Africa in which Europeans have settled, there are striking contrasts between the traditional African and the Western way of life.

Superficially, the most conspicuous symbols of difference are buildings and clothing. In Swazi areas, most of the people live in huts that are clustered together into homesteads and linked by winding footpaths. The huts are of three types, representing three main Bantu-speaking groups that have been absorbed into the Swazi Kingdom: Nguni, Sotho, and Tonga. The predominant style is set by the Nguni, the group of the royal Dlamini clan. Nguni huts are shaped like beehives with plaited ropes radiating from neat ornamental pinnacles and binding down the thatching grass. There are no special air vents, and the doorways are so low that even children have to crawl to enter. Sotho huts, which are increasing in number, have pointed, detachable roofs placed on walls of mud and wattle, or sometimes of stone; wooden window frames can be built in and there are higher doorways. Tonga buildings, which are restricted to the eastern region, have overhanging eaves as their main characteristic. In some homesteads more than one style is found, but this represents no difficulty in adjustment, no conflict in level of development. In all, the central structure is the cattle byre. The relative uniformity is maintained by the absence of special functional buildings for trade, administration, education, health or worship. The whites introduced a variety of domestic architectural styles ranging from simple brick bungalows to Hollywood-inspired mansions, and also built clearly distinguishable shops, offices, schools, hospitals, and churches. The contrast in the the exterior of the buildings corresponds to a considerable extent to differences in interior equipment and furnishings. In conservative Swazi homesteads, there are no chairs or beds. The people sit and sleep on grass mats and use Egyptian-style wooden headrests as pillows. There are no stoves, tables, or cupboards. Cooking is done on an open fire in the hut, or in the yard. Utensils are limited, and wooden meat platters and clay drinking bowls, designed for group, not individual, portions are kept on the floor, which is of stamped earth smeared with moistened cow dung, to make it smooth, clean, and sweet-smelling.

Clothing, a more personal demonstration of cultural identification than buildings, always reflects major distinctions of sex and age. Small Swazi children are decked only in narrow waistbands of beads or plaited grass, with tiny charms to protect them against various evils. Older boys flaunt their manliness behind triangular flaps of animal skins, and later wear these over materials tied like a skirt and reaching to the knees. Young unmarried girls wear gay prints tied around the hips with a separate piece of cloth knotted over one shoulder. Married women are conspicuously set apart by heavy skirts of cowhide and aprons of goatskins, so tied that it is easy, with practice, to swing a baby from the back and suckle it at the breast. Whites, particularly missionaries, condemned traditional clothing as immodestly revealing, and Western clothing became for some Swazi synonymous with "Western civilization" and a first essential of Christianity.

Striking differences tend to mask the extent of borrowing and adaptation resulting from over a hundred years of white settlement. The effects are most visible on the outskirts of urban centers developed by Whites, where Swazi live in simple Western-styled-and-furnished houses, but even in the isolated backwoods of the bush country, woolen blankets, beads, tin trunks, and bottles are conspicuous clues of contact. Perhaps most significant, although also less conspicuous, are the pieces of paper symbolizing the penetration of the written word. We find in modern Swaziland a small group eager to imitate the ways of the whites and, at the other extreme, a group that rejects all things Western and longs for an idealized golden age; between the extremes are the mass, whose choices are not consciously or deliberately made in terms of whether they are "traditional" or "Western." The need for cash crops drives many Swazi to work for long periods in the world of the whites, but they do not live there as white men, and when their period of service is over, they return to their homes, unaware of the extent to which they may have been changed by their experiences.

Very few Swazi attempt deliberately to live in both worlds at the same time. The exception to this general rule is the present *Ingwenyama*, Sobhuza II, an educated conservative, with a deep pride as well as a vested interest in the traditional culture of his people. Applying the crude cultural indices of building and clothing, we find that he is the head of the most conservative homestead in Swaziland, but that he has also bought two of the most modern houses in the country. He retains the heavy drapes and solid furniture of the original white owners in the front rooms, where he serves hard liquor, and tea from bone-china cups. The rooms at the back have acquired a more traditional atmosphere; here one sits on mats on the floor with Sobhuza's wives and drinks beer from the common bowl. Sobhuza's clothing, like his housing, mirrors a conflict of cultures. When he interviews white officials in their own offices, he wears a tailored suit and polished shoes, and when he goes visiting, he usually carries a cane and a hat. But in his own homes he dresses in cloth and loinskin and walks barefoot and bareheaded with conscious majesty. Sobhuza typifies the dilemna of many a hereditary African ruler. He is a king at the crossroads—and for him there is no green light. The clash of cultures is part of a more basic conflict between two social systems: one, a small-scale monarchy with a rather feudal economy, the other a colonial structure based on expanding capitalism.

I met Sobhuza for the first time in 1934 in Johannesburg, where we were both attending an education conference. He agreed to help in a study of his people which was being sponsored by the International African Institute. When I arrived in Swaziland a few weeks later, he arranged for me to live at the tribal capital, Lombamba, in the care of his mother, the *Indlovukati*, Lomawa. He also introduced me to his closest kin and to the national council, publicly gave me permission to attend meetings and ceremonies, and delegated one of his own trusted men to act as interpreter, cook, and liaison officer. When I visited other areas, I usually stayed in the homes of local chiefs who were informed by runners of my intended arrival. I mention the cooperation received from Sobhuza because there is little doubt that without it an anthropologist would not have been able to obtain accurate information on the kingship, especially its ritual, which is at the core of the traditional system. But it was necessary to draw informants from groups of varying status, or position, and who fulfilled different roles in the kingdom. Chiefs and commoners, men and women, specialists and laymen, adults and children, educated and uneducated, view their society from different levels, which together, make up the social whole that the anthropologist studies. Although the majority of Sobhuza's subjects are less Westernized and less educated than he is, there are a few with higher scholastic qualifications and more radical ideas of progress.

In spite of Sobhuza's friendship—in some cases even because of it—the general attitude towards me, particularly in the early months, was one of suspicion and even fear. His mother, Lomawa, a shrewd, illiterate woman, acknowledged my presence with a formal courtesy characteristic of Swazi behavior to guests, but she allowed me entry into her huts only because of her son's instructions. To most Swazi I was *umlungu,* a white, who had to prove herself before she could be received as *umuntu,* a person.

Anthropological field technique is designed to obtain the necessary information from its human laboratory, but its recognized instruments—genealogies, village censuses, case histories, texts, questionnaires—cannot be applied with the objective precision of a pure science. Each society requires its own approach, since each has its specific points of entry related to its structure and values. A basic requirement of all field work is an adequate medium of communication. Anthropologists have long recognized the importance of language as a means of controlling behavior and expressing ideas. One of the great barriers that had to be overcome in Swaziland was the absence of a common language. English associated with alien masters was never spoken by Swazi when on their own, even by the few who were well schooled in it. I had therefore to learn *siSwati* or the more widely recorded *siZulu,** a language sufficiently similar to serve adequately as the medium in schools and as the official vernacular. Both Swazi and Zulu are typical of the vast family of Bantu languages made melodious by significant tonal patterns and alliterative concords that indicate, in a complicated classification of noun prefixes, a particular outlook on things concrete and abstract, on people, and on the universe itself. People laughed at whites who spoke "kitchen Swazi" but they became interested and sympathetic when they watched me strive to acquire the "deep" language with all its nuances and melodies, and they expressed their joy when I was finally able to follow what was being said, and sufficiently fluent to take part without embarrassing my audience or myself.

In the process of mastering the language, the field anthropologist learns other essentials of social behavior and joins in various routine activities until he or she becomes a familiar figure whose presence is no longer disturbing. Gradually I broke through the fence of noncommunication, and field work became a richly rewarding human experience. In Swazi society I found all types of people—proud, humble, generous, mean, gentle, talkative, shy, lazy, industrious. I recognized old friends in new shapes so that the familiar became strange as the strange became familiar. The human matrix remained universally com-

---

* The *si* is the characteristic prefix of this noun class.

plex but the cultural imprint varied and the qualities were often differently rated. The Swazi themselves have a number of ideal personality types, and, with an increasing differentiation between the traditional and the modern, these types sometimes conflict with each other.

This case study is but an introduction to one small group of people in a so-called "underdeveloped country." Since anthropology became a recognized discipline over a hundred years ago, there have been many approaches to the study of society, each making a contribution, no one really definitive and final, each stimulated by ideas current at a particular period. The following analysis is primarily influenced by the structural and functional approaches developed mainly by British schools of anthropology. The presentation of the material would have been different had I used a purely ethnographic, or a more comparative, or a psychological approach. Though much material has been omitted, that which has been selected covers the main aspects of Swazi life—political, economic, legal, religious, and social—as expressed in institutionalised systems of behavior.

Anthropologists analyze a society at a particular period of its history, and this book deals primarily with the Swazi in the years from 1934 to 1945 when I did my most intensive field work. Shaping this period, which I will treat as the ethnographic present, was a living past—starting with the first of the remembered kings and moving dramatically, rather than historically, through the period of contact with whites until the present time. Like other Bantu-speaking tribes, the Swazi had no script by which they could transmit their past to paper, and their approach to time was episodic rather than chronological. Famine, wars, epidemics were rememberd in isolation. The major unit of time is a reign, the duration of which is obviously not as accurate a measure as a decade or century, but is an index of social time. In the reign of some kings very little occurred; under others there were major events and crises.

Swaziland in 1962 is in many respects a different society from that of 1945. Since World War II, there has been a more positive approach to the political rights, the economic development, and the educational needs of the people. These will be indicated in the final chapter in which I discuss the main trends of change and also the continuity of tradition. The material for this is based on three short visits to Swaziland (1958, 1960, and 1961), but mainly on written documents: official publications, newspaper reports, articles in scientific journals, and private correspondence.

The position is not static. Developments after 1945 have brought whites and Swazi into new alignments. Economic investments by private companies and by the Colonial government are linking some of the most backward areas into the network of international finance; the granting of independence to various African territories has set up a chain reaction throughout the continent; in Swaziland, as in other nonindependent British colonies, efforts are being made to bring European and African inhabitants into a more "modern" democratic relationship. Within the Swazi state itself, political parties have emerged with goals different from those of tribalism or colonialism. I will show in the final chapter that the structure of Swazi society is less rigid than it appeared at the end of 1945.

From Clan to Colony

Traditional History

THERE ARE SEVERAL VERSIONS of traditional Swazi history because tribal historians, generally old men interested in the past, frequently contradict each other and themselves. Anthropologists are concerned less with the accuracy of remembered details or speculative reconstruction than with the way the past is perpetuated and sanctions existing institutions.

Kingship is hereditary in the proud Nkosi Dlamini clan, and Swazi historians recall the names of some twenty-five kings, though there is agreement on only the last eight, beginning towards the end of the sixteenth century with Ngwane II, the first king commemorated in modern ritual. For a reason no longer remembered, he and a small group of kinsmen and retainers left their home on the east coast and moved inland across the mountains, an achievement recorded in the royal song of praise "Nkosi Dlamini—You scourged the Lebombo in your flight." They finally settled in what is now southeastern Swaziland, known to the Swazi as the "Place of Burning," a name that some informants say refers to signs of previous habitation. There Ngwane died, and annual pilgrimages have ever since been made to the cave in the tree-covered hill where he and his royal male kin lie buried in state.

Swazi have no flag or national emblem by which to rally group sentiment, but the names of kings and such other verbal symbols as songs of praise and anthems serve a similar purpose. A limited number of royal names are given in irregular rotation, and the names of the old capitals are also repeated, serving as links with tradition.

Ngwane's grandson, Sobhuza I, came into conflict over garden lands with a powerful neighbor, Zidze, of the Ndwandwe clan, who was also building up a following. Sobhuza is remembered as a strategist who, at all costs, tried to avoid pitched battles against powerful opposition. Rather than fight against the Ndwande, Sobhuza moved northward with his group and established himself finally in the midlands at the foot of the Mdzimba Mountains, which remain to this day the area of most royal villages. The people who accompanied him are described as the "pure Swazi," "those who broke off with the Nkosi Dlamini, at The Place of Burning," and are the nucleus of the Swazi state.

The country they entered was already occupied by people of both Nguni and Sotho stock. The Sotho spoke a somewhat different language and practiced slightly different customs, but they were not organized for warfare and their level of culture was the same as that of the Nguni invaders. From all these people, described as "The Found Ahead," Sobhuza demanded allegiance. Some came humbly, offering tribute of food and maidens; others were defeated and plundered, but once their loyalty was assured, they were allowed to continue under their own recognized clan heads subordinate only to the Dlamini king. At least one group simply moved beyond his reach. "The Found Ahead" who remained and survived were incorporated as a second group into the growing state. From them, the Dlamini ruler acquired, among other things, new and powerful magic for rain, war, and cultivation, which bolstered his military conquest by extending his range of ritual. He further consolidated his position by diplomatic marriages, and sought as his main wife a daughter of his erstwhile enemy, Zidze of the Ndwandwe. He also sent two of his own daughters to the powerful Shaka, founder of the Zulu kingdom, and maintained his neutrality even when the Swazi princesses suffered the fate of all Shaka's queens and were killed when they became pregnant. On Sobhuza's death, he left his successor a strong kingdom, respected and feared by neighboring tribes, with a centralized political system controlling several thousands of people scattered over areas reaching far beyond the boundaries of modern Swaziland.

Throughout southern Africa in the late eighteenth and early nineteenth centuries, small tribes linked by kinship were being organized into strong military states under ambitious rulers. This important change in the structure of the traditional political units is primarily related to greater economic pressure on the land. Being peasants, their existence depended on the soil, and they moved when the yield was considered too low or the area too limited. But the tribal population was increasing, and land to the south, formerly open to African expansion, was being taken by the whites. Conflict between the tribes and between Africans and whites became inevitable.

Sobhuza's heir, Mswati, by his main wife, Zidze's daughter, was the greatest of the Swazi fighting kings. Probably influenced by the successful Zulu, he reorganized his army, which before had been on a local kinship basis, into centralized age regiments, and equipped his men with the short stabbing spear in addition to the long but less controllable throwing spear. To keep order over his vast domain, Mswati established royal homesteads as mobilizing centers for men in outlying districts, and these also served as military outposts from which to launch attacks on independent tribes. His armies' raids reached Southern Rhodesia, and the name of Mswati was the terror of the north. The warriors brought their plunder to the king, who redistributed most of it, giving preference to the heroes. Important captives were sometimes exchanged for Swazi prisoners of war. Destruction of the fighting forces of an enemy did not necessarily result in the permanent extinction of the vanquished group, or in their lasting hostility to the victors. The Dlamini king emphasized the sanctity and power of hereditary leadership, and as long as a chief or the heirs of a defeated people survived, he acknowledged him as a foundation on which the conquered groups might be rebuilt as part of the Swazi state. Thus, Mswati reinstated heirs whose allegiance was assured in the district of their fathers, and in this way both extended his domain and made staunch allies of once-powerful enemies.

The disruption of rival kingdoms magnified Mswati's power. Many survivors fled to his "armpit" for protection. His fame also attracted distant relatives of established tribesmen who were anxious for a protector in this period of intertribal conflict and unrest. Some were humble and insignificant and others were powerful; Mswati established loyal groups in sparsely populated districts under their own chiefs, he placed royal princes and nominees from commoner clans in control of clans that he trusted less. The immigrants became known as "Those Who Arrived After" and form a third category in the state. Of the present clan names, totaling over seventy, approximately one fifth are regarded as "True Swazi," one seventh are "Those Found Ahead" and the remainder are "Those Who Arrived After." About 70 percent of the clans are Nguni, 25 percent Sotho and 5 percent Tonga. Every clan has its history, and the combined history of all the clans gives the mandate of superiority to the Dlamini conquerors.

The Nkosi Dlamini did not attempt to enforce their culture, and even today there are local differences in dialect, architectural style, dress, food, utensils, and ritual. But considerable uniformity resulted from the method of absorption and the participation in national affairs granted to all subjects. The groups have intermarried, all are entitled to protection, to land, to bear the national mark—a slit in the lobes of the ears, to wear Swazi costume on state occasions, to serve together in the age regiments, and to speak in the council. These privileges and responsibilities of citizenship are conferred on everyone owing allegiance to the "twin" rulers—mother and son—and cultural homogeneity is greatest in the areas closest to these central authorities.

The Paper Conquest

The initial relationship between Swazi and whites was friendly and cooperative. Informants relate that Mswati's father, Sobhuza I, was forewarned of their arrival in a dream, even before cloth, beads, and guns substantiated their existence and before news of bloody battles between them and tribes to the south spread to his people. Early in Mswati's reign, which lasted from 1830 to 1868, Boer farmers from the Transvaal came in search of better grazing for their cattle, British traders from the east coast bartered their wares for ivory and skins, hunters shot the wild game that abounded in the bush veldt, and an English missionary worked for a while in the south. Several white men visited the king himself, who received them courteously.

Though the whites came as individuals, they were not isolated. They were members of two separate and antagonistic political communities—the Boer and the British—each struggling to establish itself in a country predominantly inhabited by non-whites. Initially, the Swazi were prepared to treat either or both white groups as allies, and Mswati appealed to the English for protection against the raids of the Zulu and sent an army to help the Boers defeat a hostile Sotho tribe to the north. In return for 150 breeding cattle and services (unspecified) he also signed his cross on two documents presented him by officials of the Boers; though these documents had no immediate effect, they ceded virtually his entire country to the whites and were the precursors of the spate of concession that led to the final subjugation of his people.

Mswati's death in 1858 was followed by a period of internal strife, centering on disputed succession. Rivalry between princes for the kingship had become part of the dynamics of traditional politics, but it gave whites the opportunity to further their economic ambitions by political intervention in the guise of "promoting peace." Mswati's heir, Ludonga, was a minor and Mswati's mother (the daughter of Zidze) and one of his half brothers were acting as regents. Ludonga died suddenly and mysteriously and suspicion fell on the male regent, who was clubbed to death. Ludonga's mother had only the one son, and his half brothers, sons by Mswati's other wives, wrangled and fought for the throne. Finally one group of princes agreed to appoint the motherless Mbandzeni in Ludonga's place to rule together with Ludonga's own mother. Thereupon the Boer Transvaal Republic sent a commando of 400 men to Mbandzeni's installation; after the ceremony the leader of the Boer troops had Mbandzeni make his cross on the document ratifying the concessions granted by his father, Mswati.

Boer and British expressed different interests in Swaziland. The Boers were predomiantly farmers searching for good arable land and also for a route to the coast which would enable them to establish their own port and avoid all contact with the hated British at the Cape. They were therefore anxious to annex Swaziland. On the other hand, Britain, following the loss of her American colonies and the rise of free trade, wanted to consolidate her empire rather than expand it, and had no desire to assume added financial responsibility. She was, however, reluctant to let the Boers gain control of a country of unknown promise or divert trade from her own southern ports. Her nationals were mainly interested in mining and commerce. In 1882, gold was discovered in the northwest and hundreds of European fortune hunters entered the country. They sought personal interviews with the king, to whom they gave cash, blankets, dogs, horses, guns, gin, and other products of the "civilized" world in return for the mark which he was asked to make on the documents they placed before him.

From the time of his selection, Mbandzeni's own position in the tribe was insecure. Hostility developed between him and the queen mother and culminated in a short civil war in which he sent his regiments against her. She fled with the rain medicines, but was captured and throttled. In her place, the king's supporters appointed another wife of his father, carefully choosing a woman with the clan name of his (Mbandzeni's) own deceased mother, and with no son of her own. On two subsequent occasions, Mbandzeni executed princes whom he found plotting aginst his person. Neither the British nor Boer governments had legal authority to restrain him, having guaranteed the independence of the Swazi in two conventions (1881 and 1884). But the internal tensions expressed in the rebellions were intensified by the presence of whites. They were in the country of the Swazi king, but were not his subjects; they did not serve him, yet they employed his men as their servants; their conspicuous wealth overshadowed his possessions and he complained that each white man behaved "like a king."

Though the sovereignty of the Swazi was frequently asserted, Mbandzeni had no constitutional control over the whites and a few lawless individuals, by-products of many a frontier situation, were a threat to all sections in the country. In an attempt to deal with the situation, Mbandzeni appealed to the British High Commissioner for assistance; when his request was refused he made use of a principle of government already developed among his own people: hereditary privileges in a trusted family. He turned to Sir Theophilus Shepstone, a proven friend of Swazi kings and a man who had supported the institution of chieftainship among the defeated Zulu, and asked him for one of his sons. Thus it came about that "Offy" Shepstone, who turned out to be a young adventurer, was installed by the Swazi king as paid "Resident Advisor and Agent" of the Swazi nation, with power to negotiate all matters affecting the whites. Swazi recall with great bitterness that it was during the period of his office that the majority of concessions were granted and validated.

The concessions were economic weapons representing a type of warfare beyond the traditional system. They included laws of land ownership that clashed with rights of customary usage, claims to minerals not yet exploited, the industrial developments of a machine age, the commerce and banking of an expanding capitalist economy. A leading councilor complained: "We hold the feather and sign, we take money but we do not know what it is for."

To assist him in his economic negotiations, "Offy" also introduced into Swazi government the principle of elective, as distinct from hereditary, representation, in which special interest groups, rather than the state as such, held the balance of power. He organized the concessionaires into a committee represented by fifteen elected property owners, with five additional members as king's nominees. To this committee, Mbandzeni gave, somewhat reluctantly, a charter of self-government, expressly reserving for himself the right to veto any decisions, emphasizing that he was "still the king." But in actual fact he had lost many of the powers associated with that position and when he was near death he mourned, "Swazi kingship ends with me."

Several textbooks blame Mbandzeni for the chaos that resulted from the indiscriminate granting of concessions, and condemn him as weak and dissolute, but he is remembered by his own people as a king of peace duped by unscrupulous whites. Judgments of personalities generally involve an element of self-identification. And it is left to the more impartial observer to point out that economic and political forces are more powerful than the qualities of any single individual in shaping the course of a country's history.

The death of Mbandzeni in 1889 was followed by a period of national unrest that was intensified, although superficially restrained by the presence of the whites. Swazi attribute death to sorcerers, and it was customary on the death of a king to kill all suspects. The British and Boer governments, despite their verbal recognition of Swazi sovereignty, had previously protested against this royal prerogative; when Mbandzeni died, the Swazi queen regent requested to be allowed "to destroy for just one day the evildoers who had murdered the king." Permission was refused, and this time the national leaders "resentfully submitted to the British queen's detestation of the practice." After heated discussion, but without bloodshed, the council selected as main wife and future queen mother, Gwamile Mdluli, a woman of unusual intelligence and ability, whose eldest son Bunu was a headstrong youth of sixteen years. A rival candidate was sent far from the capital. Sporadic violence continued. Stories of Swazi atrocities were headlined in the settlers' newspapers. There was a recognized increase in crime. To responsible Europeans settled in the country or with interests there, the necessity for a single administration became urgent. The white committee failed to exercise control, and was followed by a provisional government representing Boer, British, and Swazi, with "Offy" as the Swazi nominee. Torn by national and personal rivalry, it muddled along for over three years, during which period it "confirmed" 352 out of 364 concessions, but it had neither the organization nor support for effective executive action.

In 1894—without consulting the Swazi though knowing well it was entirely against their wishes—the two white powers, Boer and British, concluded a further convention whereby the country became a "protected dependency" of the South African Boer Republic, and powers of traditional rulers were circumscribed by the formula that they should be recognized only "insofar as they were not inconsistent with civilized law and customs." Among the powers the Republic bestowed upon itself was the right to impose a hut tax on the Swazi, a technique deliberately introduced in many parts of Africa to coerce peasants who had no cash crops into the labor market. Swazi objected to pay "money to keep the white man in the country," and as the time for collection approached, there were rumors that they would resist by force and that their rulers had summoned specialists in war magic to fortify the army. Tension was high, when a leading councilor who was sympathetic to the whites was executed at the capital. The Republican authorities summoned the young king, Bunu, to appear on a charge of murder. The nation mobilized. Bunu himself sought protection from the British magistrate in Zululand. "I have fled my country," he said simply, "because Boers are invading it and bringing in arms to kill me. I have stolen no sheep and shed no white man's blood." The British intervened and after a lengthy correspondence and a most unusual trial, Bunu was fined 500 pounds sterling (approximately 1400 dollars) and reinstated; at the same time a protocol drawn by both white governments radically curtailed criminal jurisdiction of future Swazi rulers. The "paper conquest" represented by concessionaires, but ultimately backed by superior military force, was complete, and the Swazi were no longer recognized as an independent state. When, in the following year (1899), the Anglo-Boer war broke out, the Swazi nation remained neutral.

The Period of Acceptance

In 1902, Britain reluctantly took over Swaziland as an added liability of a bitter military victory. Bunu died during the war and his mother Gwamile, and a younger brother, Malunge, acted as regents. The future queen mother, Lomawa, was chosen from among Bunu's widows because she was of the same Ndwandwe clan with which Sobhuza I had made so successful a marriage alliance. Lomawa had one baby boy, who had been named Mona (Jealousy); once she was appointed, the boy was given the royal title of Sobhuza II, and he is the present *Ingwenyama*.

The Swazi anticipated that the British would restore their sovereign rights and expel the troublesome concessionaires, but these hopes were soon shattered. However, in course of time, through economic and political developments, the Swazi recognized the whites as a vital part of their world and the years of friction merge with a period of interdependence and voluntary acceptance of British control. The machinery of a modern administration developed slowly, starting in 1902 with a little police force whose primary duty was to restrain the hostility of the Swazi and collect tax. Its personnel and duties were steadily extended. In 1906 Swaziland was placed under the British High Commissioner for South Africa, and, in 1907, a full administrative staff with a resident commissioner at the head and experts for different activities was appointed.

The government realized, however, that before there could be development or security in the new multiracial milieu, it was essential that the concession issue be finally settled. So the British appointed a commission and used its findings to proclaim that one third of every land concession be set aside for the sole and exclusive use of the Swazi and that two thirds remain with the white concessionaires, who could compel Swazi living in their area to move after a period of five years. Partition was organized by a skillful white administrator who divided the "Native Areas" into twenty-one separate blocks, but drew the boundaries in such a way as to create a minimum of disturbance in the more densely populated areas. The Swazi protested verbally and without effect. All arms and ammunition were taken from them.

Whereas Mbandzeni had attempted to control the whites by techniques established in the traditional system, Gwamile and Malunge strove to regain the rights of their people through methods introduced by the whites, within the framework of a domination they realized they could no longer overthrow by force. Gwamile openly expressed the belief that money and "books" were keys to the white man's power, and she imposed a cash levy on the Swazi for a fund to try to buy back the land, and also started a school for princes and sons of leading councilors, bringing in as the first teacher a colored man from Zululand. From the little local school she later sent Sobhuza II, together with a small clique of agemates and a sister to cook and sew for him, to a mission school in the Union (now Republic) of South Africa. Here he studied, until at the age of twenty-one she publicly announced him ready to assume the role of "Paramount Chief of Swaziland and King of the Swazi nation." In a letter written on her behalf in 1921 to the Resident Commissioner to inform him that she had handed over the reins of government, we read, "This is the day I have always longed for. It has now come at last like a dream which has come true. King Mbandzeni died in October, 1889, thirty-two years ago. As from that day my life has been burdened by an awful responsibility and anxiety. It has been a life full of the deepest emotions that a woman has ever had. Bunu died after only a very short life, leaving me with the responsibility of bringing up his infant son and heir. I rejoice that I now present him to your honor in your capacity as head of the administration of Swaziland. He is very young as your honor can see. He shall constantly require my advice. I and the the nation have every confidence in him. I have brought him up as a Swazi prince should be brought up. His spirit is in entire accord with the traditions and feelings and aspirations of his countrymen, and what is more, I have given him the opportunity to obtain the very best training which any native youth can obtain here in South Africa. Sobhuza II gets his name, title and position by the right of inheritance from his ancient house and kings who have ruled over the Swazi nation from time immemorial."

Sobhuza II's first national duty was to contest the concessions in the law courts of the white rulers. A special court of Swaziland gave judgment against him. In 1922 the nation sent him to appeal to the Privy Council in London. He was accompanied on this mission by a few illiterate elders, his private medicine man, an English-trained Zulu advocate, and a representative of the Swaziland administration. The Swazi nation lost the appeal on a technicality. In his judgment Viscount Haldane stated "this method of peacefully extending British Dominion may well be as little generally understood, as it is, where it can operate, in law unquestionable." The Swazii did not understand, but had to accept.

Though much of Swazi history is unique, the general outline for the past seventy-five years has been set by the wider economic and political interests of colonialism. Modern Swaziland is the meeting ground of two separate policies, that of the adjacent Republic of South Africa and that expressed by the British Colonial Office. The South African policy of *apartheid* is openly dedicated to the maintenance of white domination; the British proclaim the priority of African interests in their own territory. Provision has existed since 1910 for the transfer of Swaziland to South Africa, and the local Swaziland administration has been strongly influenced by economic pressure from the Republic and by the presence in the country of white settlers who have the colonial attitude towards the "natives."

Within the framework of white domination, a distinctive Swazi way of life persists. The imposition of the colonial system does not automatically eliminate an existing system of kinship or kingship. On the one hand, opportunities and inducements to change have been restricted by the whites; on the other, a conservative monarchy has attempted to resist the loss of its tradition-based identity.

White Swazilanders to whom I spoke in 1961 considered that the position of the Swazi had "improved considerably" in the postwar years. They mentioned development in communication, agriculture, mining, and industry and increasing investments in education, health, and welfare. Superficially, indeed, it seemed that the Swazi were better off and more Westernized. Nearly all the men and women wore Western dress, few were in traditional clothing or in ragged castoffs, a common sight in the urban areas two decades ago. At Lobamba the administration had installed a new office and taps for (cold) water. More families owned beds, chairs, and sewing machines and several had battery-powered radios.

But what of the attitude to the bearers of these gifts? Swazi appeared to show no corresponding increase in good will. There was less superficial courtesy and more openly expressed criticism. Very few gave the customary greeting and the open acknowledgement "we see you," accompanied by the hand raised in salutation, a greeting which before had been extended to anybody, white or black, along the roadside. Old friends who felt they could speak freely complained that the whites still held most of the good jobs, even though some of their own people were equally qualified. Although the administration, acting on instructions from England, was trying to hammer out a new political constitution, a section of the Swazi were becoming politically more aggressive (or progressive?) and anti-white.

The implication of the Swaziland situation is clear: economic aid alone, given without understanding of the society, may create greater antagonism than friendship and more destruction than construction. Effective control of the reaction of the people requires a knowledge of their past as well as present society and a recognition of what the people themselves want for their own future. Change is a process that may take a number of different directions; the anthropologist can offer no single formula for progress and must recognize that "happiness" is the most elusive of evaluations.

2

Kinship and Locality

Clan, Lineage, and Family

IN THE PREVIOUS CHAPTER we observed the historical process whereby people of different clans were welded into a centralized state, a political unit, by a conquering Nguni aristocracy. In this chapter we shall consider the working of the kinship system. In most small-scale personal societies, kinship by descent and ties by marriage influence behavior in a great number of situations; they determine where and with whom a person lives, his range of friends and enemies, whom he may or may not marry, the positions to which he is entitled.

The clan is the furthest extension of kinship, and when two Swazi meet for the first time they soon ask, "What is your *sibongo* (clan praise name)?" This is a major initial identification. Every Swazi acquires by birth his father's clanname, even if his mother is not legally married and her child is cared for by her own people. Women retain their paternal clan name on marriage but may never transmit it to their children.

Swazi clanship regulates marriage and, to some extent, political status. I will deal with the political aspects first, as I have already indicated that a centralized monarchy replaced the heads of autonomous clans. In the process of centralization, members of the royal clan spread throughout the territory and most clans are no longer distinct local groups.

Clans are graded roughly according to the relationship they have with the kingship and the position their members hold in the state. At the apex is the Nkosi Dlamini, in which the lineage of the king is pre-eminent and the closer the blood ties with kings, the higher the status of individuals; next in rank come clans described as "Bearers of Kings," that is, clans that have provided queen mothers who were as a rule chosen because they were the daughters of powerful chiefs. Third in rank are clans with their own local areas and hereditary chiefs, which have not yet provided queen mothers. Slightly below them are clans from which officials are selected for special ritual or administrative functions, and finally come clans with no coordinating clan ceremonies, no local centers, and no recognized national representatives.

The grading of clans is neither as precise nor as static as a caste system. Grading does not depend on differences of custom or occupation and is not maintained by endogamy (in-group marriage) nor sanctioned by the concept of ritual pollution. On the contrary, differences of customs are tolerated, there is no clan specialization of occupation, exogamy is the rule, and interclan contact is free and intimate. But the upper limits of promotion are set by the royal Dlamini clan.

Clanship is of primary importance in regulating marriage and succession. Marriage with a person of one's own clan is prohibited except for the king, the only man permitted to marry a clan sister. Inbreeding to the point of incest is a royal prerogative in many aristocratic societies; among the Swazi, incest between the king and a sister is both openly hinted at and condemned in one of the most moving of the sacred songs sung at the annual ceremony of kingship. At the same time, clan exogamy is recognized as an effective way of extending and creating social ties, and the king is expected to unify and centralize his position by taking women from all sections of his people. When he marries a clan sister, her father is automatically removed from the royal Nkosi Dlamini clan, and becomes the founder of a separate subclan. This also limits the number of Dlamini; a nobility always tries to maintain itself as an exclusive minority.

Subdivision of clans is a widespread process, dating from the early period of migration when brothers hived off, each with his own small group of followers who identified themselves through the name of their new leader or with an incident in their more recent history. The link between them and the parent clan is retained in additional praise names (*sinanatelo*), and intermarriage is prohibited. Only among the Nkosi Dlamini do we find the deliberate creation of separate subclans for the purpose of intermarriage, but the king's clan sister will never be selected as his main wife; the future queen mother is always chosen from an outside clan.

Each clan contains a number of lineages in which direct descent can be genealogically traced over three to eight generations. Swazi lineages define legal rights and claims to various state positions, but do not provide the framework for the political structure as they do in certain segmentary societies, which have no centralised rulers. Kinship reinforces local ties but the two are not identical. Evidence of an original local basis to the clan and the lineage is found in the changing meaning of the word *sifunza*. In reply to the question "What is your *sifunza?*" Swazi usually give the *sibongo* (clan praise name), but when asked "Who is the chief of your *sifunza?*" they generally name their political chief, though his *sibongo* is different from their own, or they give the name of the man they consider the direct successor of the founder of their clan, even though he lives in another locality.

Swazi clan and lineage structure emphasizes the agnatic* kin as distinct

---

* Agnatic (noun agnates) is kinship through the male line only; sometimes termed patrilateral.

from the elementary family, in which relationship with both parents is recognised. However, kinship always involves some theory of descent, some explanation of conception. Certain matrilineal societies deny the physical role of the male, and interpret birth as the result of a sort of immaculate conception, or impregnation by a clan "spirit" or totem. This is not the case with the Swazi, who stress the physiological link between father and offspring and state emphatically that a child is "one blood with its father and its mother." The king in particular must have in his body "the blood" of kingship through the male line. The biological tie between father and child must be confirmed by law and ritual, for the physiological father (genitor) is not automatically the sociological father (pater).

Rights of fatherhood are acquired through *lobola,* the transfer of valuables, especially cattle, from the family of the man to that of the woman. If no *lobola* has been given or promised, the child remains with the woman's family while she, herself, may be separated from her offspring and given in marriage to a man other than the genitor. But the child retains the clan name of the genitor, the physiological father, who may among the Swazi—but not in neighboring tribes—*lobola* his offspring, even if he rejects its mother.

When a Swazi woman is in labor, she is asked the clan name of the baby's genitor. If she is not married she gives the name of her lover and the matter is fairly straightforward—either he gives *lobola* and takes her and/or the child, or the child remains with her parents and she is married elsewhere. But if the woman is married and she knows that the begetter of her child is not her legal husband, she must still confess. Otherwise it is believed that birth will be hard and may even prove fatal, for the child belongs "by blood" to the clan of the genitor, but by law to the man who gave the marriage cattle. Adultery by a woman was formerly punishable by death of both guilty partners, partly because it was a violation of the husband's basic rights over his wife, and partly because it was a threat to his group to "mix the clan names" through a woman acquired by the group.

The most important daily interaction takes place in the family environment of the homestead, where children are born and cared for, play and learn, and adults lead their private lives. The structure of the homestead is more flexible than that of clan or lineage and its composition fluctuates with births and marriages, deaths and migrations. Swazi distinguish between kinship ties and homestead ties. The homestead is an area of common living, and though ties of kinship and membership in a homestead usually reinforce each other, kinsmen trace connections through blood or marriage.

In control of the homestead is the patriarchal headman (*umnumzana*), whose prestige is enhanced by the size of his family and the number of other dependents. A conservative homestead may include the headman, his wives, his unmarried brothers and sisters, married sons with their wives and children, and unmarried sons and daughters, as well as more distant relatives. Among all southern Bantu, polygyny is regarded as a social ideal rather than a sexual extravagance, and because of the importance of payment of *lobola,* only the aristocrats and wealthy (and often elderly) commoners are able to achieve many wives. The king has the royal prerogative to take by force (*qoma*) girls he desires who are not yet betrothed, but he must exercise his privilege with some restraint. In 1936, Sobhuza, then thirty-five years old, had some forty wives; by 1961 he had married eight additional women. Girls chosen by the king are publicly recognized as future queens with political potential. Many wives are primarily symbols of status, and their children build up the lineage of the father and the size and influence of his homestead.

The Homestead Plan

The homestead is built according to a definite plan that reflects the main interests of the occupants and their status relationships. In the center is a heavily palisaded, unroofed cattle pen, and, if the lay of the land permits, its main gateway should face the rising sun, a symbol in family and national ritual. Men and boys have free access to the cattle byre but women may only enter on special occasions. Dug into the cattle byre are deep flask-shaped pits for storing the best grain from the fields. Informants state that the pits were devised in the days of tribal warfare to hide food from the enemy, and the fenced cattle byre served also as a stockade against attack. At present, siting the main granaries in the byre enables the headman to keep some check on the food supplies used by the wives.

The king's homestead follows the same basic principle as that of any established polygynist but is on a larger scale and has a greater elaboration of ritual symbols. The enormous cattle byre at the state capital is the meeting place of all the people, and at the upper end is a sanctuary where the king is periodically "doctored." This doctoring insures his status—it bestows on him the requisite personality, described by the word "shadow," and the ingredients required for the king are more potent (and secret) than those permitted to any subject.

Grouped round the western end of the byre are the living quarters. Among many southern Bantu there is a rigid placement of wives in order of rank, but this is not the case among the Swazi. The only fixed point is the main enclosure with the "great hut" (*indlunkulu*) under the charge of the mother of the headman, or, if she is dead, of a sister co-wife, or, in special cases, a wife who is then raised to the status of "mother." The "great hut," often decorated with skulls of cattle sacrificed to the headman's ancestors, is used as the family shrine: in the rear, the headman offers libations of beer and meat. Places and things that are sacred must not be approached by any person who is considered ritually "unclean"; among the Swazi, menstruating women, people in mourning, and adults "hot" from sexual intercourse are never allowed to enter the *indlunkulu*. The shrine is specifically dedicated to the headman's senior paternal relatives, a category of kin towards whom younger female in-laws in particular must show stereotyped respect. In some of the more conservative homes, the wives of the headman make a detour to avoid passing in front of the doorway, or they deliberately avert their eyes and drop their voices when they approach. Though they may not enter the sacred hut, they are made conscious of its presence and of their own exclusion each time they gather in the yard of the "mother" (their mother-in-law) to perform common chores and discuss domestic routine. While daughters-in-law must avoid the "great hut" out of respect, their children may even sleep in it, entrenching the legal and religious distinction that is drawn between the patrilineal in-group and the women brought in from outside. The "great hut" at the capital, a magnificent structure, is periodically repaired by materials contributed by tribal labor and retains in its framework ropes and mats handed down from one reign to another. Inside, hidden by a reed screen, are sacred relics, including types of grain no longer grown; the huge dome is supported on heavy poles of ritually treated wood, and above the doorway are tiny holes through which the king spits in times of special celebration, symbolically radiating creative essence. Here, he and his mother speak to the royal ancestors on behalf of their subjects and perform the rites to bring rain.

Distinct from the huts of the "mother" are the quarters of the wives. In ordinary large homesteads, after a period of service to her mother-in-law each wife is given her separate sleeping, cooking, and store huts, which are shut off from the public by a high reed fence. Within her enclosure, spoken of as "the hut of so-and-so," she leads a certain private existence with her own children, who, although legally bound to the patri-kin and an integral part of the wider homestead, are emotionally most closely identified with their own mother whom they describe as "the mother who bore me." She is also allotted her own fields, and, if possible, cattle for her use, so that her "hut" is a semi-independent social and economic unit. Legal and ritual restrictions on a woman's rights are to some extent compensated for by the recognition of her economic and personal importance. A conservative headman uses his mother's hut as his daytime base and is expected to divide his nights equally between the wives. A modern headman generally has his own hut, to which he calls the women when he desires them. Among the co-wives there is frequently jealousy for which the Swazi, as other southeastern Bantu, have a special term—*ubukhwele*.

The arrangement of "huts" of the different wives facilitates the subdivision of a polygynous homestead. A headman may establish a smaller homestead for one or more wives, especially if they have grown sons, in order to obtain a wider choice of garden land, or to prevent friction between the women or (and this applies particularly to chiefs), to extend political influence. The mother's enclosure, with the "great hut," remains the main homestead, the place of ritual.

The king's wives are distributed at several royal homesteads that are strategically placed throughout the country. At the capital they live in a communal enclosure with a single narrow gateway in the high surrounding reed fence; instead of each wife having her own huts, a number of senior queens share their huts with attached junior co-wives. At the entrance of the royal harem is a hut associated with the king's marriage to his first two official wives—"the wipers away of his boyhood dirt." Like the shrine hut, this hut has been transformed from a profane to a sacred building by elaborate ritual, and it is also used as a guardroom by a trusted man especially appointed to look after the queens. The king has a personal sleeping hut deep in the harem, to which he summons his queens when he visits the capital.

Special sleeping arrangements are made for children in the homestead to conform with the expressed norm that the sex life of brothers and sisters and of parents and children must be kept separate. Young children sleep with the grandmother. Adolescent girls move into huts behind their own mothers and their brothers build barracks at the entrance of the homestead. A room of one's own is considered antisocial, and unattached individuals are always accommodated with people of their own age and sex. At the capital, the majority of the population consists of unrelated dependents who live in a double row of huts surrounding the quarters of the queen mother and of the queens. The inner row is occupied by men of rank and special office, the outer mainly by ordinary subjects who pay allegiance direct to royalty. Protecting all the civilians of the capital are men permanently stationed in regimental barracks.

Homesteads are so closely identified physically and spiritually with the occupants that the idea of selling or renting to strangers is new and repugnant to traditionalists. When a headman dies, he is buried at the entrance to the cattle byre. After a lengthy period of mourning the old site is abandoned, but the family home is revived (literally "awakened") in the vicinity by the main heir, whose duty it is to perpetuate the patrilineage. The old huts, apart from the death hut, are physically transferred to the new site and the spirit of the deceased is brought to the new family shrine. The old site, with its beacon of gravestones, becomes a treasured and fertile field for cultivating crops, which the new headman and his mother will disperse in hospitality.

Here is one example from the homestead of the late Prince Ndabankuku, an important chief in the south of Swaziland. In 1936, he had ten wives, six of whom were in his main homestead, Ehletsheni ("The Place of Whispers"), three at Mpisamandla ("Strength of the Enemy") and two at Enkungwini ("In the Mist"). Ndabankulu's mother was dead, but a co-wife of his father was in charge of the great hut. The women at Mpisamandla included Ndabankulu's first wife and her married son, but all important occasions were commemorated at Ehletsheni. Enkungwini was established to "waken" a homestead of Ndabankulu's own father, when one of his (Ndabankulu's) married sons wanted to move from Ehletsheni in order to obtain more land for cultivation. It was considered natural that the boy's own mother, La Simelane, one of Ndabankulu's senior wives, move with her son and daughter-in-law, and that they cultivate the fertile site of an ancestral homestead. Ndabankulu sent with La Simelane a younger wife, a full sister who had been "put into her marriage cattle" and given by the parents as *inhlanti* (junior co-wife) to her older sister. Ndabankulu died a few years ago and I am told that the council chose the senior Simelane sister as his main wife. It will behove her son to send some of his wives to "waken" Ndabankulu's other homesteads should they be left without close members of the family.

The king, in particular, must "waken" the main homesteads of his royal predecessors as well as inaugurate a series of his own. He perpetuates the old homesteads by sending some of his wives to live there, and one of their sons will become the chief prince of the area. In each reign the village of the ruling queen mother is the capital of the state; in relation to it, the king's personal homestead, established after he has taken his first ten queens, is described as the men's quarters or the "barracks."

The search for a site for a new homestead is guided partly by material considerations, the availability of adequate land, water and wood, and partly by social factors. A Swazi seeks friends, preferably kinsmen, as neighbors, and also seeks a chief with a good reputation. Should he find that he has chosen badly—as indicated by the unaccountable failure of crops or the sudden illness of his children, or unnecessarily frequent demands for his service—he will move with his family and his property to a more congenial social environment. Although his physical needs are important, it is even more essential for him to live among people whom he trusts. He does not necessarily sever his connection with the main branch of his kin, and he recognizes the heir as representative of the lineage, with the right to appeal to the ancestors on behalf of all its members.

Throughout Swazi areas, homesteads are said to be decreasing in size, partly because there is no longer the need for physical protection against man and beast and also because new interests, economic and religious, are cutting through the relatively closed and self-sufficient domestic groups of patri-kin. But the homesteads of aristocrats still tend to be larger than those of commoners, and the homesteads of non-Christians larger than those of Christians. In a sample area in the middle veld, the average number of occupants was over twenty-two in the homes of aristocrats and seven in commoners' homes. The largest homestead is obviously the queen mother's; the smallest I saw belonged to a Christian widow, living with two unmarried sons, far from their nearest kin. Such an isolated group, not even a single complete family, is a modern phenomenon. It is unusual, except in urban townships, for an elementary monogamous family to live on its own without contact with kinsmen in nearby homesteads. Similarly, it is only in European employment centers that unattached Swazi live anonymously outside a domestic circle.

Types of Marriage

Swazi marriage is essentially a linking of two families rather than of two persons, and the bearing of children is the essential consummation of wifehood. Swazi marriage is of so enduring a nature that should the man himself die, the woman is inherited through the custom of the levirate by one of the male relatives of the deceased to raise children in his name. Similarly, since the production of children is the essential fulfillment of the woman's part of the contract, should she prove barren her family must either return the cattle or, following the custom of the sororate, provide her with a relative, preferably a younger full sister, as junior co-wife to bear children to "put into her womb." For the second woman, no extra *lobola* need be given.

Divorce is rare in Swazi society and it is particularly difficult for a woman to be legally permitted to marry a second time. The reason for this is not to be sought in the amount of *lobola* but in the institutional complex of patrilocal marriage and the power of the patrilineage expressed through such customs as the levirate and sororate. High *lobola* is a symbol, not a cause, of the permanence of marriage. The amount of *lobola* varies with the woman's status. Twenty years ago, it ranged from twelve head for a commoner to as many as sixty for an important princess. Several head cattle are contributed by representative headmen throughout the country for the woman who is chosen as the main wife of the king.

Lobola is a controversial issue in modern Africa. Uninformed administrators and missionaries regarded it initially as "the buying and selling of women" and attempted to abolish it by law, but the tenacity with which Africans, including Christians, have retained the custom has led to a reinterpretation of it at a deeper sociological level. *Lobola* is generally translated as "bride price," but it is clear that a woman is not regarded as a commodity by the people involved. On the contrary, she is a valued member of the community, and her past status and future security are symbolized in the transaction. By giving *lobola,* her children are made legitimate and become entitled to the benefits of the father's lineage; by accepting *lobola,* her people are compensated for the loss of her services. Their emotional ties and ritual obligations towards her do not cease, and should she be ill-treated or find herself and her children destitute, she may appeal to the recipients of the cattle, who will be legally, as well as morally, obliged to assist her. The husband does not acquire a chattel, but a wife for himself and a mother for his children, and he and his kin owe her definite obligations of support and protection. In urban areas of southern Africa, money is being substituted for cattle; the mercenary aspect of the negotiations is being exploited by some unscrupulous parents who marry their daughter to the highest bidder and who, because they are remote from the extended kin, do not fulfill their traditional parental obligations. But even many educated urban women are not prepared to be married without the passing of token *lobola* in addition to Christian and civil marriage rites.

Swazi practice several types of marriage, and these are important in determining succession and inheritance in polygynous families. Selection of the successor, who is also the main heir, depends on the rank of the women in the harem. Among the Swazi aristocracy the first wife is never the main wife. Seniority in marriage brings certain advantages during the headman's lifetime, but upon his death other factors are considered. The most important is pedigree, and the daughter of a king or leading chief generally takes precedence over all other wives. There are also marriages with specific kin, of which the most important in Swaziland is marriage to a woman who has the clan name of the man's own paternal or maternal grandmother. The reasons for this will appear later.

These so-called "preferential marriages" are generally arranged by the parents, and arranged marriages, which are not necessarily forced marriages, always bestow a higher status than those based solely on individual choice. Swazi, however, recognize the power of personal attachment, and if a man informs his parents that he wishes to marry a particular girl, they may willingly send a representative "to beg a fire" from her people. Should they agree, the full marriage ceremony is performed, and her character may win her recognition as the main wife. The woman who has least chance of being selected is one who "makes love for herself" and runs to the man's home against her parents' will. Though the man's group claims her openly as a daughter-in-law, she is at a disadvantage because of the fact that her family opposed the marriage. If they did not accept any *lobola*, she may be given as wife to another man. Sometimes a grown son gives *lobola* for his own mother in order to legalize his status in the wider patrilineage.

The traditional marriage ceremony dramatizes an underlying tension between the two intermarrying groups and the necessity to create certain permanent bonds between them. Throughout the elaborate and formal series of rituals, the woman's family must display its reluctance at losing her. Her mother weeps and tells her to behave with restraint in the husband's home though she be subject to unaccustomed restrictions and accusations, and her father asks the ancestors to protect and bless her in the midst of her in-laws. She leaves her home accompanied by a group of supporters, including "brothers" and responsible elders appointed by the parents, who remain behind. The man's group receives the bridal party with warmth and friendliness, but the girl must neither smile nor respond. In one of the most dramatic moments of the ritual, she stands in the cattle byre of her husband and mourns in song the loss of her girlhood freedom and cries to her "brothers" to come and rescue her from her fate. They have been hiding and rush to her assistance in a demonstration of family loyalty and unity. In a mock battle carried out with much apparent fierceness, they rush off with her in their midst. But the girl knows, and they know, that she must finally accept the role of woman as wife and mother, and she returns when her future mother-in-law calls her back with a promise of a cow. Later she is smeared with red clay, signifying the loss of her virginity, and a child from her husband's group is placed in her lap as a promise of future motherhood. In the end, she ceremonially distributes gifts of blankets, mats, and brooms, brought from her home to the various in-laws whose favor is so necessary for her future happiness.

The marriage ceremony, which lasts several days, culminates in a feast at which an ox provided by the groom's group is divided, each family receiving half. When the bride's group returns, they leave with her a young girl to ease her initial loneliness, and the new wife is gradually introduced to the responsibilities of her new status. The following winter the groom's people bring the cattle for her marriage; her people pretend to drive the cattle back, but after this mock demonstration they make the "in-laws" welcome and may ever promise to send a second daughter as a junior co-wife. Once the bride has borne her first child, she is more often called "mother of so-and-so" than by her own distinctive clan name.

Basic Behavior Patterns

It is in the homestead that the main members of the Swazi family, husband and wife, parent and children, grandparents and grandchildren, brothers and sisters play out their roles in dynamic interpersonal relationships. Their behavior is patterned by the mating and kinship system; these—and not any psychological quality per se—account for the differences in the behavior prescribed for a Swazi father or mother and a father or mother in other societies.

Swazi classify kin into a limited number of broad categories, embracing with a single term relatives who, in more specialized and isolating societies, are kept distinct. Thus, the term "father" is extended from one's own father to his brothers, half brothers, and sons of his father's brothers. Similarly "mother" embraces his own mother, her sisters, her co-wives, and wives of his father's brothers. The children of these "fathers" and "mothers" are his "brothers" and "sisters," and their children are grouped in the same category as his own grandchildren. The use of a common term does not mean that a particular key relationship is unimportant. Indeed, within the category there are usually accurate descriptions of degrees of closeness. "The father who bore me" is distinguished from "my big father" (my father's older brother) or "my little father" (father's younger brother), but one's behavior towards all "fathers" is modeled on a single pattern.

A Swazi soon learns to separate in word and action the relatives of the father from those of the mother. They are two distinct legal groups, and so strong is the identification through one or the other parent that the word for father's sister is literally "female father," and the mother's brother is "male mother." Towards the "female father," a Swazi behaves with the respect and obedience associated with the word "father," and towards the "male mother" with the affection and familiarity evoked by "mother." The children of my "female father" and "male mother" are included in a single term, which can be translated as "cousins," and they are treated in a different way from "brothers" and "sisters." Each kinship term is thus like a mnemonic, reminding the person with whom he or she may sleep, eat, or joke, who must be respected and who avoided.

Implicit in the system of terminology is the assumption that kinsmen covered by a single term share a common social identity and, in some situations, can serve adequately as substitutes for each other in case of need, an assumption tenable only in societies where specialization is limited and where greater importance is attached to the kinship group than to the individual. This is the reality behind such customs as the levirate, in which brothers are regarded as equivalents, and the sororate, in which sisters may replace each other to fulfill specific wifely functions.

No equality is expected or desired between Swazi husband and wife. He is the male, superior in strength and law, entitled to beat her and to take other women. She must defer to him and treat him with respect. But a Swazi woman is not an abject and timid creature; she claims her rights as "a person" as well as "a wife." Should her husband maltreat her severely, she has no hesitation in berating him and, if necessary, running off to her people; she may, and very occasionally does, lay a charge against him before the "white man's court." Her people generally send her back for they are not prepared to return the marriage cattle, but they do inflict a fine on the husband for his offense. His behavior is also largely controlled by the constant supervision of his senior kinsmen, who are interested in the security and extension of their lineage, and by the pressure of his own mother, who depends on the services of her daughters-in-law. There is generally severe censure by a woman's kin as well as by her in-laws if she complains to the alien law of the whites.

An outstanding feature of Swazi kinship is the father's authority over his children. The term "father" is associated with someone who is both feared and respected. The headman is the "father" of the homestead. The king is the "father" of the country. The most direct and permanent power is wielded by a father over his own sons, who are legally minors even after marriage, until they establish separate homesteads, and formerly could not marry unless he provided the cattle for their wives.

Swazi men may never treat their sons as equals, even if they should wish to do so. Between father and son there is a conflict of institutionalized interests. A son is consciously recognized as a potential threat to the father's position, though, at the same time, he is necessary to perpetuate the father's name in the ancestral cult. Perhaps their relationship contains an element of the classical Oedipus complex, the unconscious rivalry for the woman as mother and as wife. The complicated rules of succession attempt to regulate the conflicting interests of father and son. The first son of a polygynous home is never the main heir. He is his father's confidant and helps him maintain authority. His mother takes precedence over later wives in such matters as distribution of food, but her son should never be allowed to challenge the father's position or to replace him. In polygynous families the heir is never publicly appointed until the father is dead. Conflict between the father's and son's generations impinges at the deepest levels—sex and life itself—and in many patrilineal societies there are institutional devices for minimizing contact. Among the Swazi, married sons are expected to live in the homestead of the father, but between the sons' wives and their father-in-law there is the strictest avoidance. They must not look each other in the face or use each other's names, and the women must use a special language of "respect" in order not to mouth any word with the name or even with the main syllable of the name of the father-in-law or of other senior male in-laws.

The legal authority of the father is in contrast to the more indulgent relationship with the mother, for whom Swazi men express affection and appreciation, as well as respect. A well-known riddle runs, "If your mother and wife were drowning, which one would you save?" The right answer is, "My mother. I can get another wife but not another mother." Swazi say, "The desires of men are satisfied by women but the satisfaction of women comes through their children."

In this patrilineal patriarchal society, there is even less personal intimacy between a father and his daughters than between him and his sons. Not only are they separated by sex and age, but a daughter leaves the home upon marriage and produces children for another lineage. The legal and economic aspects dominate the father's behavior, whereas the mother, herself an outsider, is said to "feel for," and to "share the sadness" of the girl and is expected to intercede on her behalf, both before and after marriage. In recognition of the mother's services, the family that is benefiting by her daughter sends with the *lobola* cattle a special beast known as "the wiper away of tears." This is the mother's private property; it is given for each daughter and is inherited by the mother's youngest son, a stereotyped darling.

Behavior between siblings, as this last point illustrates, is influenced by seniority and sex. Older siblings take precedence over younger, males take precedence over females. This is shown in the laws of inheritance. The main heir, who is always a male, inherits the bulk of the family property, including the cattle attached to the great hut, but the eldest son of each independent wife takes the *lobola* of his own sisters—except for the animals which belong to the youngest brother. Middle sons may inherit nothing, but they must be helped with marriage cattle before their juniors. The marked inequality of inheritance frequently causes rivalry between brothers and half brothers. Girls, who can never inherit family property, are less directly involved in family disputes. Swazi men have nothing to fear from their sisters and much to gain from them. It is their cattle that enable the boys to obtain their own wives; hence, when a sister visits her married brother, she must be treated as a most privileged guest and must be waited on by his wife, her sister-in-law, whose possessions she may use freely. The brother's children are told to fear this woman, the "female father," more than their own mother.

In addition to parents and siblings, grandparents are also integrated into the intimate world of the Swazi child. They teach the young to respect their parents, but their techniques are proverbially more lenient. Grandparents "scold by the mouth," parents "more often with a stick." Because marriage is patrilocal, children frequently grow up in the homes of the paternal grandparents, but, especially in cases of illness or tensions, children may be sent to stay for long periods with the mother's people. Lineage obligatons are reinforced by the paternal grandfather, the man whom the father himself must obey, while emotional protection is expected from the maternal grandparents who express their interest in the daughter's child, described as the "child of the calf," by a series of ceremonial gifts.

The conflict inherent in the parent-child generations is absent between grandparent and grandchild. Grandfather and grandson are, in fact, recognized as allies with mutual interests in curbing an overambitious and authoritarian individual, the son of the former, the father of the latter. Grandson and grandfather are culturally removed from sexual conflict, and the grandson is, to some extent, identified with his grandfather and given authority to regenerate him. This, Swazi say, is the reason that a marriage between a man and a woman of the clan of his grandmother is considered desirable.

We have already indicated that behavior between blood kin is different from behavior between in-laws. Patrilocal marriage separates a man from his wife's relatives, who live in their own homestead; but towards his senior in-laws, particularly his mother-in-law, he must show respect and avoidance, comparable to restrictions imposed on his own wife towards his senior male relatives. He may not eat, swear, or relax physically in the presence of his mother-in-law; but, being a male, he has certain privileges denied to a woman, and he is not restricted in language and movements to the same extent. On the rare occasions when he visits the village of his in-laws, he is treated as a distinguished guest and provided with all possible delicacies.

Behavior towards other members of the in-law group depends largely on whether they will be prohibited from marriage or permitted to marry. Thus, in sharp contrast to the avoidance enjoined between a man and his mother-in-law or his wife's brothers' wives, who are potential mothers-in-law, is the familiarity demanded of him toward his wife's sisters. Swazi say that the love between sisters overcomes the jealousy between co-wives; to take a wife's sister as a junior wife is provided for in the marriage ceremony itself.

In traditional Swazi society, kinsmen provide an ever-increasing network of social relationships, and in different situations people behave in stereotyped ways set by ties of blood or marriage. In the urban areas, where Swazi are isolated from the wider circle of kinsmen, they are still intensely aware of the need for people of "one blood" to assist in such crises as illness, accidents, or funerals. Clan brothers may then become substitutes for real brothers, and fictional kinship may be built up with people who come from the same neighborhood. The specialized interests that form the basis of association in more complex societies are still few in Swaziland, and it is mainly relatives who cooperate in work, ritual and government.

3

Political Structure

THE SWAZI were not conquered by force, and though the functions of traditional authorities were changed, the political system with its network of kinship was ostensibly allowed to continue under the British administration. It is only in very recent years that a deliberate effort has been made to integrate the dual monarchy into a Western democratic framework and to develop a single government for the entire territory of Swaziland.

The traditional statuses of the king and queen mother remain conspicuous in their daily routine. Both receive elaborate deference: their subjects crouch when addressing them and punctuate royal speeches with flattering titles. He is "The Lion," "The Sun," "The Milky Way," "Obstacle to The Enemy." She is "The Lady Elephant," "The Earth," "The Beautiful," "Mother of the Country," and so forth. Compared with them, the highest tribal officials liken themselves to "stars" and "ant heaps," and the average commoner speaks of himself disparagingly as "a dog," "a stick," "a nothing." The rulers are always accompanied by attendants and are set apart by unique regalia. The queen mother wears a crown of dark-brown wooden pegs, topped with a bright red feather of the flamingo, the rain bird, set between two lucky beans; around her ankles and wrists are tied small pouches of animal skins containing royal medicines. The king has less conspicuous insignia, except on special occasions when he appears in dazzling and startling robes. Both are regularly treated with "the medicines of kingship" to give them "shadow," (personality). The well-being of the nation is associated with the king's strength and virility, and he must neither see nor touch a corpse, nor approach a grave or a mourner. The major episodes in his life—birth, installation, marriage—are heavily ritualized. Death ceremonies, which always reflect the social status of the deceased, vary from the insignificant burial accorded the child of a commoner to the elaborate state funerals of rulers. The king, and the king alone, is embalmed by a primitive method known only to a clan that "broke off" with the Dlamini at the original home, the "Place of Burning."

The traditional Swazi constitution is complex, and, in some respects, extremely subtle. Superficially, all powers—legislative, executive, administrative, and religious—center in the *ingwenyama* and *indlovukati*, but tyrannical exercise of their powers is restrained by their own relationship, by a hierarchy of officials whose positions depend on maintaining kingship rather than on supporting a particular king, by a developed system of local government, by councils of state, and by the pressure of subjects who formerly could transfer their military strength and support to rivals. Among the neighboring and more military Zulu, hereditary succession was tempered with assassination. The structure of Swazi kingship restrained despotism.

The first check on the abuse of power and privilege by rulers is contained in the dual monarchy itself. The king owes his position to a woman whose rank—more than his own personal qualities—determined his selection for kingship, and between the two rulers there is a delicate balance of power. He presides over the highest court, and, formerly, he alone could sanction the death sentence, meted out for witchcraft and treason, but she is in charge of the second highest court and the shrine hut in her homestead is a sanctuary for people appealing for protection. He controls the age regiments, but the commander in chief presides at the capital. He has power to distribute land in the "native area," but together they work the rain magic that fructifies it. Sacred national objects are in her charge, but are not effective without his cooperation. He is associated with "hardness," expressed in thunder, she with the "softness" of water. He represents the line of past kings and speaks to the dead in the shrine hut of the capital; she provides the beer for the libations. He is revitalized in the annual ritual of kingship, which is held at her home. He is entitled to use cattle from the royal herds, but she may rebuke him publicly if he wastes national wealth. In short, they are expected to assist and advise each other in all activities and to complement each other. In the past, when the nation was more homogeneous and both rulers were "illiterate," their duties were evenly distributed, but today the king is educated and shoulders more of the administrative responsibilities, letting the burden of ritual fall primarily on the queen mother.

Conflict between the king and queen mother has always been recognized as a potential menace to national security and well-being, and certain rules, not always obeyed, have been formulated over the years in an attempt to minimize tension. Temperamental differences are appreciated in a society built on a personal kinship basis, and as the king is chosen by virtue of his mother's rank, there is a possibility that she might favor another son more than the heir. To avoid this, the rule for royalty states "A king is not followed by blood brothers," that is, the queen mother should have only one son. Once appointed, no matter how young she may be, the queen mother is prohibited from bearing additional children; and when her husband dies, she is excluded from the custom of the levirate that applies to all other widows. Direct conflict is also avoided by the compulsory spatial separation of the king's village from the capital. The queen mother is not allowed to move far from the national shrine, and she may spend weeks without a visit from the king. Diplomatic intermediaries carry messages between them, eliminating friction that might be engendered by face-to-face arguments.

Swazi assert, "A king dies young." His mother is expected to train her successor and hand over power when the new king reaches maturity. According to Swazi idiom, "The pumpkin plant lasts beyond the fruit"; that is, the queen mother outlives the king. In the present reign, this did not happen. Sobhuza has lived longer than most Swazi kings. His own mother, Lomawa, died in 1942 and was replaced by Nukwase, her full sister and co-wife. When Nukwase died, the tribe was in a dilemma, and the councilors finally appointed one of Sobhuza's own senior wives from the same clan as the two deceased "mothers." This woman is now called "mother," and is removed from all wifely relationship with him. Every society must adapt to the unexpected; it does not simply cease to function because of unforseen difficulties.

In the previous chapter, we showed that the elaborate system of succession was partly a means of protecting a man against the competition of his sons. The first son of a king is never his successor, and if he marries a woman of such high rank that she will obviously be the main wife, he only takes her when he is well on in years. Guardianship, as a means of transferring power from one generation to the next, is institutionalized at the national level in the regency.

Rulers maintain their position by delegating authority to trusted officials, related and nonrelated. Nepotism, the granting of privileges to kinsmen, is an accepted principle in Swazi government, and power radiates from the king to other members of the royal lineage, who are described as "children of the sun," "eggs of the country." The more important princes are sent to districts as chiefs and serve as members of the inner council of the state. They are expected to build up the prestige of the monarchy, to report significant rumors of dissension, and to see that subjects respond to summons to national services. But Swazi history repeats a tale familiar from the cycle of English kings: where hereditary monarchy is the accepted political system, the royal lineage itself provides rivals for kingship. Important princes should never settle too near the king and their ambition should be satisfied by granting them limited local autonomy. In Swazi idiom, "There is only one king." Not only should he have no full brother, but, in this polygynous society, he must be wary of half brothers by other wives of his late father. The princes may never enter the enclosure of the king's wives, may never touch his clothing, eat from his dishes, or use the "medicines of kingship." Their relationship with him is thus essentially ambivalent. On the one hand, it is in their interest to build up the Dlamini kingship, and on the other, to prevent the king from becoming too powerful. His senior male relatives, particularly his uncles and older half brothers, are among his main advisors and supporters, and also his most outspoken critics.

Protecting the king from royal rivals and other enemies are ritually created blood brothers known as *tinsila*, (literally, "body dirt" or "sweat"). The *tinsila* are always drawn from specific nonroyal clans. The first two *tinsila*, the most important, are roughly the same age as the king, and are chosen soon after his appointment so that they may participate with him in the ordeal of puberty, in the first marriage, and other rituals marking his growth in status. Some of the king's blood, together with special magical substances, is rubbed into incisions made on the bodies of these two men, and blood from their bodies is similarly transferred to him. Thereafter, these *tinsila*, who are also metaphorically described as the king's "twins," may touch his person, wear his clothes, and even eat from his dish. The two senior *tinsila* are called "father" by the people, including the princes, who may appeal to them to intercede with the king in personal difficulties.

"Blood brotherhood" is widespread in Africa but need not be symbolized by actual blood transfusion. It is frequently accompanied by acts of commensality and oaths of mutual help. Among the Swazi the medicated blood is sufficient, but the relationship it creates is not symmetrical: the *tinsila* benefit the king more than the king the *tinsila*. Swazi believe that any attack by evildoers against the king will be deflected by the *tinsila*, whose bodies serve as his "shield." He runs less risk of being endangered by their enemies because their position is less coveted. Yet, so close is the identification of the *tinsila* with the king that should they die before him, they are not recognized as sociologically dead, and their widows, who had been selected by the royal council and married with cattle from royal outposts, may not mourn their loss till the king himself dies.

In addition to the first two *tinsila*, a series of junior *tinsila* are appointed at different times to carry out routine and intimate ritual associated with the person of the king. Thus we have a series of individuals, drawn from commoner clans, who are brought into pseudokinship ties with the king to protect him from close physical contact with members of the royal lineage.

The female relatives of the king are political and economic assets and should be judically handled as investments. The more important female relatives (paternal aunts, sisters, and daughters) are given in marriage to foreign rulers and to non-Dlamini chiefs, in whose homes they are recognized as main wives. However, because they live in the homes of their in-laws, they are able to take little active part in the central government.

Although the political structure emphasizes the male agnates of the king, the close relatives of the queen mother also influence national affairs. Her brothers, who are the king's "male mothers," usually receive posts in the central administration, if they do not already hold them, and act as intermediaries for the maternal line in certain situations of crises. On the appointment of a new king, the maternal relatives of his predecessor may lose their direct influence— which is largely due to affection and not demanded by law—but they retain their social prestige and a connection with the princes. The wives of the ruling king are recognized as "mothers of the people," but they lead fairly secluded lives during the lifetime of their husband, though their families constitute his important group of in-laws. The harmony of royal homesteads depends to a great extent on the king's treatment of such relatives and their friendship towards him.

Swazi emphasize that the king's allies are unrelated commoners. A basic principle of Swazi government states, "A king is ruled by *tindvuna*" (councilors).

In each reign there is a *big* (that is, leading) *indvuna* with a special title, translated by educated Swazi as the prime minister, who generally resides at the capital where he hears cases, announces court judgments, advises on the temper of the people, and acts as their representative. The position tends to be hereditary in the senior lineage of a limited number of commoner clans, but the state appointment is not restricted to the main heir. The quality required of *tindvuna* is "respect for people," and though an appointment rests with the king, the big *indvuna* may be dismissed only by the king in council. Through his position, the big *indvuna* obtains so deep an insight into state secrets and so great a hold over national resources that he is drawn into a web of fictional kinship with the ruling clan and treated in some respects as a senior prince, and therefore as one who requires restraint. He is entitled to eat from the dish of princes and is not allowed to marry into the royal clan. His behavior to the queen mother is closely observed, for in the past he sometimes collaborated with princes and with the queen mother against the king, and sometimes with the king against the queen mother. But the big *indvuna* himself can never aspire to kingship: he is without the legitimizing claim of royal blood. Leading councilors have younger officials, also of commoner clans, to assist in the execution of the more physically arduous tasks.

Wisdom in tribal precedence and skill in debate are important qualifications for civil appointments, but the head of the military organization must above all, be able to maintain discipline. Since intertribal warfare has been stopped, the number of military personnel has been limited and civil authorities exercise more authority over the age groups that formerly constituted the regiments. In dealings with whites, Western education is recognized as an asset and young men with this qualification are being appointed to civil posts.

The final group of traditional officials considered essential for national security are the *tinyanga* (specialists in ritual), who are drawn from selected clans and are required to fortify the rulers and the nation as a whole. There is no single high priest or medicine man able to challenge the king whose inherited ritual power is enhanced by the training and knowledge contributed by representatives of several non-Dlamini lineages.

Swazi traditional officials, civil, military, and ritual, normally hold office for life and are only dismissed for treason or witchcraft. Incompetence, habitual drunkenness, stupidity, or weakness of character are criticized, but as long as a man is considered loyal, he retains his post, and the only way to counteract his defects is to appoint capable men as his assistants. No salary is attached to any traditional post, but the men receive sporadic rewards for their service and may make claims on the rulers for certain specific requirements.

In addition to individual officials, two organized traditional councils guide and control the rulers. The inner council (*liqoqo*) is a development of the family council (*lusendvo*) and hence is predominantly aristocratic. Here, senior princes, together with the great councilor, have an opportunity to vent their opinions and direct policy. The number of members is not fixed, and rulers must continue with the *liqoqo* of their predecessors, occasionally adding a member of their own choice. The people have no say in and do not know of these appointments, and it would be indiscreet of them to inquire who the members were or their qualifications. There are no regular sessions and no compulsory reports on activities. The rulers may consult individual members privately, but when an important decision is essential they are expected to summon the full *liqoqo* and abide by its decision.

The second council is the *libandla lakaNgwane* (council of the Ngwane nation), a larger and more representative body that is composed of all chiefs, leading councilors, and headman. Other adult males (not females) are entitled to attend but are not obliged to do so. Chiefs who cannot come in person are supposed to send deputies who act as their "eyes" but may not commit their superiors.

The national council which meets in the cattle byre of the capital, is opened by a spokesman for the *liqoqo*, who tells the people why they have been summoned; otherwise there is little formality—no agenda, no order of speakers, no time limit, no political parties, no vote. Speakers who make good points are applauded, others are heckled and may be told to sit down. There is considerable freedom of speech, and the aim is to reach agreement, not to break up into closed, opposing factions. The sanction of the *libandla* is required on all matters brought to it from the *liqoqo*, but neither council has any specific platform and there is no sharp cleavage of interest between the two. Both developed in a society where communication was slow and life sufficiently unchanging not to require many sessions, new decisions, or trained technicians. It is only in recent years that different occupational groups have arisen to put forward sectional interests and that a radical political minority has advocated a policy influenced by different political concepts.

Local Government

Tribal territory is divided into a number of districts, each of which is organized on principles similar to those underlying the central government. At the head is a chief (*sikhulu*), who is either a prince, a nominee of the king, or a hereditary head of a non-Dlamini clan. In his area, he centralizes law, economics, and ritual; if his mother is alive, she shares with him the responsibilities of control and is in charge of the main section of the homestead. The elaboration on this basic pattern varies with the historical background of each district, and ritual, in particular, is most conspicuous among chiefs who were established because of their own hereditary lineage.

Within each district there is a weighing of power between relatives and nonrelatives of the chief. Paternal kin living in the chief's district provide him with his local and family councils and, in turn, benefit from his position; his *tindvuna* on the other hand, are outsiders and represent the majority of his subjects. There is always a main *indvuna* who attends to law cases and supervises district labor, and minor officials who vary in number with the size of the district and population. Local headmen, some of whom are more active than others, constitute the *libandla* of each chief and may also attend the national council.

The districts are attached to the main royal villages, either directly or indirectly, through *tindvuna* of the royal homesteads. In each case, the arrangement depends on political considerations and not on geographical proximity. Local affiliations are evident in legal disputes, in the granting of land, in the acceptance of new subjects and in the organization of labor. Chiefs who come directly under the king or queen mother may have considerable local autonomy, but their powers over their subjects are restricted by their own officials who can, if necessary, appeal to the rulers for assistance, and who are expected to report subversion. There is no formula in Swaziland comparable to the "destooling" (deposing) of a chief found in West Africa, but a chief who flagrantly abuses his positon may be reported to the king and told "to rest," and another member of the lineage appointed in his place.

Knowledge of the principles involved in government is acquired by every adult male as part of his domestic experience. In the homestead, the smallest local unit recognized in the political structure, the headman exercises towards the occupants rights and obligations comparable on a smaller scale to those of the chief. As their legal head, he is responsible for the torts of the inmates. As trustee-owner of homestead property he controls the distribution of cattle and the allocation of land for cultivation; as councilor he represents his dependents in local politics, and as lineage senior he appeals on their behalf to the family gods. When he considers it necessary he consults senior kinsmen, who constitute his family council.

The relationship between a chief and his subjects, like that between a headman and his dependents, is essentially personal—albeit not intimate. The term "father," extended from the family to the head of the homestead and to the chief of the district, conveys in all these contexts a combination of authority, responsibility, protection, and ritual continuity. The chief is expected to know all the families on his lands and is related to many of them. Every birth, wedding, and death is reported to him. He mourns at the funerals of his subjects and drinks at their feasts. He does not live in a different type of home nor does he attend a different school or church. His power is paternalistic, not despotic.

Swazi political authorities are criticized by their subjects if they are aggressive and domineering. Qualities such as ability in debate, efficiency in organizing work, and knowledge of the law are admired, but they are not considered essential for a chief because it is expected that his councilors will provide them. He is constantly reminded that his prestige depends largely on the number of his followers, and he is aware that they have the right to migrate from his district if he does not fulfill demands that they consider legitimate. On the other hand, his followers realize that existing bonds should not be lightly broken. Before moving elsewhere they must take a formal farewell, thanking their "father" with a substantial gift for benefits they have received. Especially at the present time when land is limited, a chief is careful to investigate newcomers who offer allegiance (*kukhonta*) and may refuse to accept men with bad records.

A subject is not a slave. Formerly in a category different from that of ordinary subjects (*tikhonti*), who offer voluntary allegiance, were *tigcili*—mainly children captured in war. *Tigcili* were taken into the homes of the rulers and leading subjects, who were described as their "owners," but *tigcili* could not be sold or killed. Moreover, there was no barrier to intermarriage, and there is no section of the population today that bears any stigma of "slave descent." *Sigcili*, however, remains a term of contempt, indicating that a person is without the security of a kinship group and has limited independence.

Swazi make no mention of slave raiding in their traditional history, although Arab slavers on the east coast influenced much of African history before the arrival of Europeans. Chattel slavery was part of the economic structure of early white colonists in southern Africa, but it was abolished before the white man settled permanently in Swaziland. The closest existing analogy is the control exercised by white farmers in the Republic over squatters on their land, a control that stops short of the actual selling of a person and is more similar to feudal serfdom. The squatter must perform compulsory service for a set period, and has no freedom of movement. Freedom to move is a primary characteristic of the traditional legal rights of Swazi citizenship.

Law and Justice

Like all southeastern Bantu, the Swazi have a highly developed legal system and a graded hierarchy of courts that coincide roughly with the political structure. Swazi stress the importance of "the law" in regulating social relationships. Private matters ("dirt of the home") are dealt with by the headman, his mother, and his senior male kinsmen; disputes between unrelated people are discussed in the first instance by the family councils of the litigants; if they cannot reach a settlement, the complainant reports to his chief, who sends him with a representative to the chief of the defendant and the case is tried in public. If this court does not settle the matter satisfactorily, either party may appeal to a higher political authority. Certain cases may go direct to the capital, others to the highest tribal court, presided over by the *ingwenyama*. In every court, each man acts as his own advocate and any male present may take an active part in cross-examination and so influence the decision. Precedents are frequently quoted, but the main concern is to unravel the complicated interplay of interests involved in each dispute and arrive at a satisfactory settlement. No oath is administered, but a man may voluntarily swear by the name of a kinsmen or a ruler, and perjury is a recognized offense.

Swazi distinguish between private wrongs, for which compensation must be given to the injured party, and cases "with blood," in which compensation is given to the king as representative of the state. Theft, slander, adultery, and property disputes fall into the first category and are punished with fines; murder and witchcraft belong to the second, and usually carry the death penalty. The death sentence is immediately executed, and the possessions of the deceased confiscated ("eaten up"). An offense against the rulers, through their person or property, is more heavily punished than one committed against any ordinary subject.

Contact between Swazi and whites is accompanied by an efflorescence of new legislation that penetrates even the more routine activities. Not only are crimes and civil offenses that were formerly covered by traditional law formulated in terms of the dominant white culture but regulations are required for an entirely new range of situations—taxation, licensing, wage employment, fencing of land, inoculation of cattle, et cetera, et cetera! Some laws and regulations apply only to whites, some only to Swazi, others to both, and, since justice itself is relative to a particular culture and is never absolute, the same laws sometimes receive different interpretations. Liquor offenses, tax evasions, breach of masters' and servants' contract constitute the highest proportion of Swazi convictions by the courts of the white administration, but these acts are not morally condemned by the Swazi. Moreover, the diviner, or witch-finder, the superior detective of criminals in his own society, is himself defined as a criminal under the Witchcraft Ordinance and can be arrested as a murderer (see Chapter 7). Case records reveal points of social tension, and legal statistics indicate the extent of social maladjustment. Breach of law occurs in every society, and some form of social sanction is essential for the maintenance of an established order. In Swaziland—as in other colonial societies—law is also used to perpetuate and enforce racial pluralism.

Two distinct legal systems, traditional and Roman-Dutch, are administered through a series of parallel courts, which interlock at certain levels. In some cases, Swazi litigants may exercise choice of court; in others, the limits of jurisdiction are defined. The superiority of white courts is not automatically accepted. Disputes over property, eviction from land, and complaints lodged by women are believed to receive more sympathetic (but not more equitable) hearing in courts presided over by white magistrates. This can be illustrated by a summary of one of numerous cases I recorded in 1936 in the court of Chief Ndabankulu. An elderly woman, Velepi Hlatshwako, and a man, Alpheus Shongwe, were brought before the chief's court, charged with "soiling the law," and fined. It appeared that about twenty years before, Velepi had been given in marriage to a man named Isauk Mabuzo (who was also present). The marriage had been unhappy: he accused her of misconduct and laziness; she accused him of ill-treatment. After a particularly violent dispute, he had "tied up her kit" and sent her from his home. This did not necessarily mean that he was relinquishing her altogether, but it was a demonstration of the extent of his displeasure: he wanted either the return of his cattle or the assurance that his wife would reform. Instead of returning to her father and reporting what had happened, in which case every effort would have been made to reunite the couple, Velepi "stole herself" and went to Alpheus Shongwe, who had been her lover before she married Mabuzo. Shongwe, the present defendant, was eager to keep her and sent a message to her parents offering bride price. They refused, saying they could not accept *lobola* twice. Her father (since deceased) and other members of his family council tried to persuade her to return to Mabuzo, but in vain. At that stage, Shongwe could have approached Mabuzo with an offer of cattle "to break the stomach" (that is, break his (Mabuzo's) relationship with Velepi), but instead Shongwe and Velepi moved to another district and let the matter ride. Mabuzo himself made no further effort to regain his wife until her daughter, fathered by Shongwe, was ready for marriage; then Mabuzo claimed both women under the terms of his original marriage payment. Shongwe, Velepi, and their daughter had become converts to the Wesleyan church, and, on the advice of the minister, went to the district commissioner to "state their case." The commissioner, a young man, summoned Mabuzo to the court house and publicly rebuked him for his "mercenary approach." Mabuzo went back to his chief, Ndabankulu. The chief and his court summoned numerous witnesses and unravelled the intricate details. This court agreed that Mabuzo was morally as well as legally in the right. Velepi had disobeyed her father and her husband, and she and Shongwe had gone "over the head of the chief" by appealing to the district commissioner. It was obvious that Mabuzo was entitled to any marriage cattle for the girl and that women like Velepi "soiled the law."

Knowledge of tribal law and court procedure is part of the normal experiences of most Swazi men, who are expected to attend discussions held in the yard of the chief's homestead, and to "talk cases" with friends and acquaintances. The formality and technicalities of the European court present a sharp contrast to tribal procedure; conservative Swazi have stated that in the former, the question of wrong and right is of secondary importance, that "the only way to win" is to have a smart lawyer.

Changing Alignments

The traditional Swazi constitution, which grew organically and is verbalized by elders, is deliberately being replaced by a new written constitution. Deliberate constitution making is not a fundamental innovation, but is restricted by the limits of a society in which there is no separate legislature and most changes come about unobtrusively through court judgments arising from specific conflicts. Swazi laws, rooted in precedents drawn from a relatively static society, are validated by reference to the past: "They were in the beginning" or "They were from the ancestors." Contact with the more heterogeneous society of whites created what has been described as "a legal vacuum" and formulae are required to deal with new situations in politics, economics, education, and health. This is part of a familiar pattern of social change in which a small-scale society, characterized by interpersonal relationships, must adapt to a more complex and anonymous outer world that requires greater specialization at both the local and international level. In all colonial systems power moves downwards, and British policy in Swaziland is directed from the Commonwealth Relations Office in Britain through a high commissioner (representing the Queen) in South Africa, to a local resident commissioner, who acts as the link between the Swazi on the one hand and the settlers on the other. From this point, power is divided between district commissioners and traditional chiefs, each with their associated personnel. Not until the late 1950s was there an effort to integrate the traditional authorities into a single bureaucracy.

The entire territory, occupied by whites as well as Swazi, is divided into three major districts and subdistricts. Unlike tribal subdivisions, these are units of administrative authority that have no essential political cohesion or loyalty, and their boundaries can be altered without consulting the inhabitants. The administrative officer in charge has no permanent roots in the country and no land to distribute to kin and followers. When he is transferred he leaves his house and his office to an unknown successor and relinquishes all ties with the people and the place. His office duties are both more general and more specific than those of tribal chiefs. He acts as a magistrate, revenue officer, tax collector, coordinator of various technical departments in the area, and as liaison officer between traditional authorities and white settlers. His post requires nontraditional qualifications—a relatively high standard of education, a knowledge of written law, a minimum of clerical efficiency, and administrative ability. Promotion depends mainly on individual achievement (academic or legal qualifications and some fluency in the vernacular) and not on claims of kinship and pedigree. Swazi draw a sharp distinction between "chiefs of the office" and their own "chiefs of the people." In Swaziland, "chiefs of the office" are white, and therefore—the argument runs—speak differently, act differently, live differently, and think differently from "the people," but not from "other whites." The majority of Swazi do not realize that even if the conspicuous difference of color did not exist, the duties and qualifications written into the position of "chief of the office" would create a bureaucratic officialdom distinct from the traditional chiefs.

Africans employed in the white-controlled bureaucracy have an ambiguous status and often conflicting roles. A few Swazi, mainly men of tribal standing, have been specifically recommended by the traditional rulers to serve as assessors to the "white" courts or as advisers to the district commissioners. They are paid by the administration, but their field is limited to matters affecting their own people and their primary loyalty is to the traditional society whose mores they must explain to the whites. In a separate category are clerks, teachers, agricultural demonstrators, cattle guards, and other technical staff that are selected, appointed, and paid by the white administration; their qualifications are formulated by Western standards, with the emphasis on education, training, and efficiency. Although these individuals derive their positions from the whites, their color keeps them outside the world to which their white colleagues return as the sun sets. Some accept this, but an increasing number resent it, and are among the more articulate of the emerging opponents of colonial rule.

Conflict is inherent in changing societies where hereditary chiefs are used as representatives both by their own conservative subjects and by the new administration, each of which represents different values. In other parts of Africa, the position has at times become sufficiently tense to prompt the colonial government to depose chiefs who expressed the opposition of their own people.

In Swaziland there has been less arbitrary action, but the position of the Swazi king *cum* paramount chief has long been the focus of opposing systems. In the first period of contact the whites exaggerated his rights and powers to obtain concessions for themselves; later, they curtailed the substance of traditional authority but used the king indirectly to act as the primary agent in bringing about his people's acceptance of innovations. At present, Sobhuza is still expected to be the first to improve his stock, use new agricultural techniques, employ demonstrators, encourage creameries and dairies, patronize schools and hospitals, and so forth. Until the early forties, he alone had regular and formal contacts with senior members of the white administration; these gave him a greater semblance of power than he actually wielded, with the result that his subjects tended to blame him for legislation for which he was in no way responsible and about which he was sometimes not even consulted. He and his mother were the only two members of the traditional hierarchy who were paid by the administration. He received 1250 pounds sterling (approximately 3000 dollars) per annum and she 500 pounds sterling (approximately 1200 dollars), which amounts were obviously inadequate for any national undertaking, but described by some Swazi as an attempt to "buy the kings."

During the war years, an effort was made to introduce the Swazi into fuller administrative, judicial, and financial control. The model selected was Nigeria, under the policy of indirect rule, and three basic proclamations—the Native Authorities Act, the Native Courts Act, and the Native Treasury Act—were eventually passed. But the Swazi situation was fundamentally different from that in West Africa where the European or white population was virtually restricted to an administrative cadre. In Swaziland, the country was owned largely by whites, and even when additional powers were granted to the Swazi by the British government, the white settlers remained a distinctive elite, with entrenched economic privileges, high status, and close ties to white officialdom.

4

Work and Wealth

The Work Cycle

SWAZI ARE TRADITIONALLY PEASANTS who cultivate crops, keep cattle and other domestic animals, hunt, and gather numerous wild fruits and vegetables. The main crops are maize and millet; in addition, every Swazi homestead produces subsidiary foods—ground nuts, gourds, sugar cane, and pumpkins.

Economic activities follow the rhythm of the seasons. The women begin by hocing and sowing small plots along the river banks where the soil is generally moist and seeds germinate quickly. With the coming of the rains in September, men and women move to large inland fields which the men prepare with ox-drawn plows. Heavy rains are expected in the summer months, from November to January, and the last gardens must be planted. In midsummer, agricultural work is intensified and communal work parties, especially for weeding, are frequent. During the day, the homesteads are emptied of able-bodied adults, and even the young children toil in the fields, often returning home in the late afternoon. In autumn, from February through March, women cut the ripe maize and tie it into bundles, then carry it home on their heads, or the men cart it on ox-drawn sleds, the main means of transport. In winter, from April through July, after the last maize is harvested and the millet gleaned, the scene of activity changes again from the fields to the homes. Men and women rub and beat the corn from the cobs and thresh and winnow the millet, reserving the best quality for storage in the underground pits and using the inferior grain for immediate consumption and to reward workers with beer.

Other activities are fitted into the agricultural cycle. When the harvest is in, people have more leisure and sociability increases. Women take the opportunity to visit their parents and headmen attend more cases at the chief's courts or relax with beer drinks. Only in the dry season, once the danger of lightning is past, may new huts be built and old ones repaired. Winter is also the hunting season, and the time when government officials go on their tax-collecting tours—with a resulting increased exodus of recruits to white labor centers.

Many Swazi live at a precarious subsistence level; their food supplies fluctuate annually between plenty and a scarcity bordering on famine. Winter is the time of general satisfaction and physical well-being, but in summer, before the new crops ripen, comes the moon named "to swallow the pickings of the teeth." Maize and millet, the staple cultivated foods, are the main commodities purchased from trading shops; it is estimated that at least 25 percent of the Swazi do not grow enough for their domestic needs. Milk and meat are also prized, but the milk yield of Swazi cattle is low; milk, preferably soured and thickened in calabashes, is eaten primarily by children; beer from sprouted grain is the substitute in adult life. Beer and meat are considered an ideal combination, but cattle are seldom slaughtered. A wide range of wild leaf vegetables, roots and fruits, and various types of insects are enjoyed, but these are unreliable additions to the starchy diet. A few nutritious items of food are culturally excluded from the entire population or from specific sections thereof. Fish was never eaten by conservatives; specific birds and a few animals are taboo to associated clans; eggs must not be eaten by females; and a married woman may not take milk in any form in the husband's home unless a special beast has been allotted her. Christians do not follow the traditional food taboos and many women converts eat eggs, buy fish, and are prepared even to take milk in public; but on the whole, the diet is unimaginative and, according to nutritional standards, badly balanced. There is no difference in the quality of food available to different status groups and the desire is to feel (and *look*) replete.

Formerly, the Swazi were entirely dependent on the land for their livelihood, and the power the rulers wield over their subjects is still referred back to their rights to allocate land. Swazi say that land, the basis of subsistence, is "served" to the people by their political overlords, and every man has the right to eat. Individual ownership through freehold and leasehold are alien concepts; rights are secured by allegiance and usage, not purchase or rental. Should the subject leave the area for several years, his land reverts to the chief, but if their mutual relationship was good, it may be reclaimed when he or his sons return. In most of southern Africa, Africans are prohibited from buying land, and there is developing a class of landless peasants who live and work on white men's farms or whose homes remain in native area, but who obtain their food requirements with money wages. In Swaziland, it is still relatively easy to find adequate building sites, but there is an increasing scarcity of fertile, arable soil. Land is open for purchase, irrespective of color, though so far most purchases have been made by the nation, through a special fund. The majority of Swazi are still reluctant—or afraid—to own land individually and to exercise a power associated with chieftainship.

Swazi have a very limited knowledge of agriculture, and, compared with the peasants of Europe or some of the Bantu tribes in central Africa, are unenterprising farmers. They recognize a few types of soil, but are not very careful in their selection, and though they realize that cow dung fertilizes the ground, they do not bother to carry it to the gardens; they do not rotate crops or practice irrigation, and "doctoring of seed" and shifting cultivation are the limits of technological effort. Cultivation is not a prestige occupation, and, as among all southern Bantu, is left primarily to the women, whose main garden tool is still the iron hoe. The introduction of the plough was probably as radical an innovation into southern Africa as that of the horse among the Plains Indians. Since handling cattle is taboo to women, the plough drawn by oxen directly involved men in the essentials of cultivation, changing the division of labor and, in some areas, the attitude to agriculture itself. Swazi have begun to grow cash crops, especially tobacco and cotton, and to form farmers' associations. Group and areal differences in response to agricultural improvements can be related to both personal and structural factors, including the character of the local chief (conservative or "forward looking"), and the relationship with the local representatives of the agricultural department, especially the agricultural demonstrator. Land allocated to and cultivated exclusively by women is not regarded as a source of cash income.

Swazi have no objective measure of area, and the size of the plots attached to each homestead depends primarily on the supply of resident labor. Women, who receive their gardens from their husbands upon marriage, may obtain occasional assistance from work parties of kin and neighbors. The rulers have several "gardens of kingship" in different localities, cultivated for them by chiefs in the area, and they are also able to command the service of regimental age groups stationed at royal homesteads, a privilege shared by district chiefs over local contingents.

Sites for building and for cultivation are individually allocated, but grazing lands are communally used. The general approach of conservatives is that land which has not been specifically altered by the efforts of man remains under the control of the political authority for the use of his people as a whole. Hence, such materials as reeds for fencing, grass for thatching, and indigenous trees for firewood, are available to all people in the district. Hunting lands are similarly controlled by chiefs, who organize communal hunts.

Cultivation provides the staple food of the Swazi, but pastoralism is more highly rated. Swazi have the so-called "cattle complex" typical of many tribes in eastern Africa: cattle, in addition to their direct value as a source of food and clothing, serve as potent symbols in a wider range of situations, both economic and ritual. They are the conservative's closest approximation to currency, his highest reward for service, his means of ratifying marriage, the medium for propitiating ancestors, and essential requirements in various treatments for health and prosperity. Their physical presence is necessary for most national and family rituals; a man without cattle is therefore considered poor and insignificant and has been likened by informants to "an orphan without kin." The slaughtering of a beast, its division and preparation, is one of the most important social situations in which status and kinship bonds are literally carved in the carcass. Each portion of the animal is allotted to set groups of individuals in terms of sex, age, and relationship; there is no personal preference permitted for choice parts. The distribution and consumption covers several days, generally culminating in the cooking of a special dish made from the blood mixed with grain and shared between men, who eat in the cattle pen, and women, who sit in the yard of the hut of the headman's mother. The over-all importance of cattle is reflected in the language, which is rich in terms for hides of different colors, horns of many shapes, and organs of animal anatomy. Men are referred to in terms of cattle and cattle are praised with the praises of men. The king is "The Bull" of the nation.

Cattle are unevenly distributed, and although every Swazi has a claim to land, he has no equivalent claim to livestock. Formerly, men could obtain cattle through inheritance or the marriage of sisters or daughters, or as gifts in return for particular services. Rich men may lend beasts to people in need, who may use the milk and be rewarded with a calf when the other animals are required by the owner. At present any wage earner may gradually accumulate a herd, but the cattle of kingship, the cattle of the nation, still far exceed those of any single individual. This national revenue is derived from several sources —inheritance, death dues for important headmen, gifts accompanying requests for rain, "thanks" for favors received, fines, and especially the marriages of princesses, and also of daughters of unrelated subjects (often royal warriors) whom the king previously assisted with their marriage cattle. I calculated (in 1936) that the royal cattle numbered over 3,000; the total cattle owned by Swazi was counted as 334,000. Through its compulsory "dipping" against specific diseases, the white administration keeps accurate vital statistics of cattle (more accurate than of the human population), but the records do not reflect actual ownership; cattle of kingship are often registered in the names of special herdsmen, and poor men are registered as "owners" of borrowed cattle. In the past, national revenue was mainly derived from loot in warfare or from the "eating up of the cattle byre" of wealthy and ambitious subjects condemned as traitors or wizards. Several royal cattle posts were established by previous kings and represent capital investment of a pre-monetary period. Each cattle post has its own name, history, and place in government. The animals are used to feed the people at national gatherings, to obtain wives for princes, or to provide beasts for national sacrifices. There is one sacred herd to which mystical properties are attributed, and which provides fat used only for anointing the king, his mother and his first two ritual wives.

Cattle circulate primarily through marriage, and cattle and wives together are the traditional hallmarks of status and the indices of wealth. In Swazi society, wealth follows the curves of natural increase and may fluctuate considerably in a man's lifetime, not through the artificial manipulation of the exchange or as a result of training, concentration, thrift, and industry, but through "good luck" or "bad luck." Death and sterility are economic as well as social threats. Swazi political leaders, because of their favored position in a polygynous and aristocratic society, have more opportunities than their subjects to recuperate from economic misfortunes. The white administration, through its veterinary department, is attempting to reduce the numbers and improve the quality of Swazi-owned cattle by experiments in pasturage, cattle culling, and organized cattle sales. Some Swazi are responding, but conservatives remain reluctant to commercialize cattle. The conflict between the traditional and Western attitudes is subtly expressed in the remark of a fairly educated Swazi: "I only like to sell cattle when I speak English." In addition to cattle, Swazi also keep sheep, goats, dogs, chickens, and, in some areas, horses, but these have not the same importance in the ritual or economy. Informants state that their forefathers had fat-tailed sheep as well as cattle before the whites arrived, and it is significant that sheep is the animal that is taboo to all members of the royal clan. Animal husbandry in general is carried on at the expense of agricultural development. Until recently, approximately 75 percent of native area was devoted to grazing and only 10 percent to cultivation, the remaining 15 percent was not suitable for either purpose.

Division of Labor

Tribal (peasant) economy has little room for specialists, and the main criteria for division of labor are sex, age, and pedigree. Every man, irrespective of his rank, knows how to build, plow, milk cattle, sew skins, and cut shields; every woman is able to hoe, thatch, plait ropes, and weave mats, baskets, and beer strainers. Swazi attach value judgments to activities over which one or other sex claims a monopoly by reason of assumed psychophysical attributes. Specific "masculine" tasks that carry high status include warfare (possibly the *raison d'être* of original male mastery), animal husbandry, and hunting. Men are also the important public figures, the orators and councilors, and the family priests. A woman's life is restricted by domestic activities, the rearing of children, and the regular chores of grinding grain, carrying water, cooking foods, smearing the floors with cow dung. Men and women cooperate in agriculture and building, but the man's share is more spasmodic and energetic, the woman's more monotonous and continuous.

Age has a less defined influence on the division of labor. Children are encouraged to do the same work as adults and relieve their mothers of certain tasks in the home. It is only in relation to ritual that age becomes a primary qualification. Immature girls are required to help in the national rain rites, and in the ceremonies periodically organized to drive pests from the crops; old women are similarly considered ritually pure and given specific tasks.

Rank by birth cuts across distinctions of age and sex so that every Swazi does not participate to the same extent in manual labor. Aristocrats and leading councilors are responsible for providing suitable conditions for the success of the efforts of others rather than their own labor. They arrange for specialists to treat the land and seed; they summon men and women for work parties in district and national enterprises; they supervise the feeding and entertainment of workers when a task is complete. They are not, however, exempt from work with their subjects, and most of them perform a certain amount of service for the rulers. On occasion some chiefs have displayed long fingernails with obvious pride, but even the most noble women, including the queen mother, are expected to take part in cultivation.

Close personal relationship between the workers and the rulers as well as between the workers themselves contrasts sharply with the legal and economic behavior of employer and employee in Western industry. There are no fixed periods of work, no regular hours, and no stipulated pay. An age set may be summoned for several days in succession, but sometimes weeks will elapse without any demand for its services. No man is forced to work, though if he consistently shirks his obligations, his mates may reproach him and belabor him with sticks. It is frequently impossible for members of a homestead to do all the work required for their subsistence without extra help; as there is no special class of laborers, they rely on kinsmen and neighbors, organized into temporary labor associations. When members of both sexes are present, they are divided into two competitive groups, spurring each other to greater achievement. Swazi generally sing as they work, their movements coordinated through music and rhythm. Every joint economic activity has its own sets of songs, and the song leader is the closest approximation to a foreman or timekeeper. The number of work parties and their size depends on status and, to some extent, on the nature of the undertaking. There are occasional large-scale national enterprises, which require considerable planning and foresight and involve as many as a thousand workers on specific days. For the organizer, a work party is both an economic venture and an occasion for the enhancement of prestige. He or she—for women may also initiate the enterprise—must calculate whether supplies are sufficient to feed the workers. The reward of communal work in conservative homes is always food, beer, or meat, eaten at the home of the host. This is as integral a part of Swazi economy as money payment in European service. But the host, unlike an employer, offers sporadic hospitality, and the food is not regarded as a wage or a means whereby people hope to support themselves. It is a way of expressing thanks, a reward to be shared among the workers according to rank, age, sex, and locality. Individual effort or piecework is not considered. Some workers come early, others late. There are well-known shirkers who enjoy the feasting without having contributed their labor, but they are aware that if they shirk too frequently, they, in turn, will not receive assistance. The work party is, in some respects, the antithesis of a trade union, and an administrative instruction from the British government to introduce trade unions into Swaziland met with the criticism from conservatives that this was a device to compel laborers to work for a definite period of time at a fixed rate instead of on a personal and voluntary basis. Traditionally, there is no sharp division between employer and employee, and reciprocity was the most powerful sanction in maintaining Swazi economic organization.

Specialization

As a result of the economic homogeneity of Swazi society, each individual plies a number of crafts, but recognition of individual aptitude has led to a limited specialization within the general skills expected of each person. Some men are better than others at tanning the hides (used for shields and for skin skirts and aprons worn by conservative married women), and some women are more skilled than others at beadwork basketwork, and plaiting mats, and so may be asked to produce these, at a price, for the less skilled. There is a marked tendency for all goods to be commercialized at the present time. Prices vary, and bargaining is not part of the Swazi convention of exchange, as it is in oriental communities. The main source of income for women who have no special skill and do not have outside employment is the sale of home-brewed beer, on which the profit may be as high as 100 percent, but the smallness of economic venture is indicated by the fact that the capital involved, if the grain is bought, is seldom more than 30 shillings (less than 5 dollars!).

The term *tinyanga* is applied specifically to specialists in ritual—medicine men and diviners—but may be extended to smiths, woodcarvers, and potters, whose crafts tend to be specialized and hereditary and involve unusual "power," and risks requiring ritual protection.

The roles of medicine men and diviners and their relationship to the supernatural will be more fully discussed in Chapter 5. Here we are concerned with the economic aspect, for these *tinyanga* have the greatest opportunity of acquiring wealth by individual achievement. Payment varies with qualifications and the nature and success of the treatment. A medicine man of good repute receives an initial gift of a goat, spear, or other articles to "open his bags," and a further payment to make the medicine "shine." During treatment he receives the hide of any beast that is slaughtered, and he is liberally provided with meat. If the patient recovers, a cow is given in thanks, but if no cure is effected, there is no final fee. For other services, such as the "pegging down" of a homestead against evil-doers or the purification of a homestead after lightning has struck, payment may be a goat or a bag of grain. A diviner's fee depends on his technique and the seriousness of the situation, but generally specialist services receive no regular stipulated payment. Sometimes the amount is decided in advance; at other times new requests are made in the course of treatment. Not to pay an *inyanga* is dangerous because of the supernatural powers he may evoke if angered. As in other societies, payments incurred by illness can cripple a family for life, while successful medicine men flourish. The amount of time *tinyanga* devote to their practice depends on personal interest, but Swazi do not regard even this exclusive profession as a substitute for peasant farming.

Smithing, which includes both smelting iron from the rock and forging it into shape, was formerly the most exacting and remunerative of the crafts. The finished articles, especially iron hoes, knives, and different kinds of spears (the main weapons of war), were in great demand and short supply. Smithing was a hereditary occupation requiring long apprenticeship and surrounded by taboos. The smithy, with its flaming forge and elaborate bellows of goatskin, was built a distance from the homestead, and women were not allowed to enter. Rich iron deposits west of Mbabane are at present being exploited by white mining companies, and Swazi smiths find it more convenient to use scrap iron and to repair old articles rather than create new ones, which can now be bought at trading stations. Certain iron instruments are sacred, and these are kept for state rituals.

Swazi claim that at one time they also had specialists in copper and brass. Substantiating this are the large brass beads, handed down from one reign to the next, that adorn the skirts of the first ten wives of the king, and a copper bracelet that is also part of the royal insignia. But if the process of forging copper was once known, this knowledge has long since been lost.

Wood carving is limited to essentially functional objects, especially headrests, milk pails, meat dishes, and spoons. There are no masks or sculptured figures, though the bushveld is rich in indigenous timber. The carver has no special status comparable to that of medicine men or even of smiths, nor is the appreticeship in any way restricted. Woodcraft is encouraged in the schools and a small tourist trade is being developed.

Pottery making survives as a special craft of women who, using the coil technique, produce different sizes and shapes of drinking and cooking vessels of considerable beauty and symmetry, decorated with simple geometrical designs. The kiln is a hollow in the ground, covered with dry brush; because it is difficult to control the heat, breakage is high. As in other situations where there is an element of risk and technical control is limitied, the Swazi potter resorts to various magical aids which in fact limit the development of effective technological improvements.

Markets comparable to those found in West Africa do not exist in Swaziland, but a certain amount of internal trade follows the irregular distribution of raw materials. Wood carvers, especially, are concentrated in bush country, and some of the best clay is found in riverbanks in the northwest.

With Westernization, a range of new, full-time occupational situations have been introduced. Some 12,000 Swazi males are employed mainly as unskilled laborers in farming, mining, building, and transport, and some 1,000 women are also in farming and domestic service. A much smaller number (under 500 men and 200 women) are teachers, clerks, and messengers, and there is a growing number of Swazi, mostly men, in "self employment" as shopkeepers, butchers, and "agents." New jobs associated with school education carry more prestige and a higher standard of living than those that do not require "writing." But as yet there is no economic class division, and the few educated men and women in financially good positions have not cut adrift from the extended family; the majority of their kin are both uneducated and unskilled peasants, and are often migrant laborers.

Wealth and Status

Accumulation of wealth is not conspicuous in traditional society, where rulers and subjects live in the same type of home, eat the same kind of foods, and use the same limited range of utensils and implements. The perishable nature of most Swazi products as well as the limited range of choice, make generosity the hallmark of achievement and the primary virtue of *ubuntfu* (humanity). From infancy, children are taught not to be greedy or to take too large a portion of food from the common pot, and they, themselves, soon enforce the rule of sharing. A mother who hides food for her own offspring will be insulted by co-wives and suspected of witchcraft, and the character of a headman is judged by his hospitality. A donor must always belittle his gift, while the recipient must exaggerate its importance and accept even the smallest article in both hands.

Begging has a connotation different from that expressed in the European milieu. Among conservatives it carries no shame. To beg is a sign of deference and to give is a token of superiority, enhancing status. It is the person who refuses a request who should suffer; to avoid inflicting shame, borrowers express their requests through intermediaries and the refusal should be couched in self-deprecatory terms. Something given in response to a request is a favor and need not be returned. It is totally different from objects that are specifically borrowed and also from those that are bought and for which there is an obligation to pay at a later date. A person is thanked for a favor by the further request, "Do the same tomorrow."

Inequality of wealth has always been acceptable but only within the aristocratic framework. Commoners who acquired too many wives or cattle were in danger of being "smelt out as evil doers," for whom death was the penalty and whose property was legally "eaten up" by chiefs. These drastic measures are prohibited by modern law, but in the rural areas there is still considerable restraint on ambition and ability. Rich conservatives divide their homesteads, lend out their surplus cattle, bury their grain in underground pits, and hide their money in the ground. The fear of witchcraft acts as a check on economic enterprise, and it is safer to plead poverty than to boast of wealth.

Although display of wealth is limited in traditional circles, a large range of trade articles has made economic differences more conspicuous, and a new, white-controlled, economic milieu has redefined status. Smart suits, record players, Western furniture, and sewing machines are the prized posessions of self-styled "progressives" while Sobhuza demonstrates a new "high" in aristocratic living. But the major obvious disparity in wealth is not between traditional and progressive or aristocrat and commoner, but between whites and non-whites.

5

Age and Education

Training the Young

IN EVERY SOCEITY age is a social, not an absolute concept, measured by artificial standards correlated more or less directly with the major physiological changes of infancy, prepuberty, adolescence, maturity, and the menopause. Generally speaking, in preliterate peasant societies increasing age carries increasing responsibilities, and elders, as "repositories of tradition," exercise considerable influence and command corresponding respect. The authority of age characterizes all Swazi behavior, and age is the main factor in group association.

Swazi distinguish, linguistically and ritually, eight periods of individual growth, from birth to "almost an ancestor." Until the third month of life a Swazi baby is described as a "thing." It has no name, cannot be handled by the men, and, if it dies, it may not be publicly mourned. It is recognized as being very weak and vulnerable (infant mortality is tragically high), and the parents perform various rituals to protect it against dangers emanating from animals, humans, and from nature herself. In the third month, the infant is shown to the moon and symbolically introduced to the world of nature. It is entered into the category of persons, and is given a name, which may be sung to it in its first lullaby. It remains a "baby" until it has "teeth to chew" and "legs to run." This stage, which lasts roughly three years, is traditionally terminated by the act of weaning. Until then the baby remains most closely attached to the mother, who carries it everywhere in a sling on her back, feeds it when it cries, and tends it with devotion. Other people, including the father, may also fondle it and deliberately try to teach it basic kinship terms and correct behavior.

Obedience and politeness are inculcated from the beginning of awareness. Little achievements meet with warm encouragement and such stereotyped praise as "Chief," or "Now you are really a man"—or "a woman." Toilet training is generally achieved within the first two years without much apparent conflict. The mother abruptly removes the baby from her back when she feels discomfort, but occasional lapses are treated with tolerance. Weaning, enforced, if necessary, by the mother's rubbing bitter aloe or some other unpleasant-tasting substance on her nipples, is a symbolic as well as a real separation from maternal care.

The baby now becomes a toddler, who must begin to be independent and associate with his peers. When the mother goes to work in the fields or to gather firewood, she may leave him for many hours in the care of children not much bigger than himself, who play with him, sing to him, and teach him accepted rules of behavior. Disobedience or rudeness may provoke a sharp slap, but, as a rule, less drastic teaching by the play group appears sufficient to produce conformity. The threat of a beating is constantly uttered by both adults and older children for various "mistakes," but is seldom carried out.

Discipline becomes more strict and punishment more physical as the child grows older, but the over-all impression is that Swazi children are reared with unself-conscious indulgence, relatively free from constant adult supervision. They also learn unconsciously through riddles and verbal memory games, said to "sharpen the intelligence," and there are songs and dances to "make a person grow into a person." Most of the play of children is based on the activities of the adult world. Small boys model clay oxen (today some model automobiles) and indulge in stick fights. Girls pretend to grind and cook and do each other's hair. Children of both sexes build miniature huts near the homestead and act out the roles of kinsmen. In the evenings, the old women in whose huts they sleep after weaning recount tales and fables which, though ostensibly meant to entertain, frequently point out a moral. Legends dealing with clan and tribal history are recalled on specific ritual occasions.

At about the age of six, Swazi children have a small slit made in the lobe of each ear. They are no longer protected toddlers; they are now held more responsible for their own actions. Control of tears and laughter is part of the stereotyped process of growing up, and though the ear-cutting operation is quite painful, the children must bear it bravely. Thereafter they are encouraged to participate in economic and social activities insofar as their physical strength permits. The education of boys and girls is differentiated in accordance with the male and female roles in this society. The training of boys is directed towards hardening them physically and bringing them into public life. They must be severed from the womenfolk and "must not grow up under the skin skirts of their mothers." They go in small gangs to herd the calves in the neighborhood and are later promoted to the herding of the cattle, during which period they spend much of the day away from their homes, acquire a knowledge of nature, and learn to fend for themselves. The girls, on the other hand, are allowed less freedom of movement. They accompany their mothers or agemates to draw water or gather wood, or plant in the fields, and much of their time is spent working in the home where they help with the cooking and smear the floors. But a Swazi girl, like a Swazi boy, has an easy life before marriage, with much time for singing and dancing, recognized essentials of social life.

The attainment of puberty is a major landmark in individual development but is not publicly celebrated. Group circumcision of boys was practiced

until the reign of Mswati when the custom was abandoned. It appears that the mortality was high and the military needs of the nation were considered more important than the ritual of personal transition. A symbolic circumcision, however, is still performed for the king as part of the ritual of his installation. There are no initiation ceremonies for girls, but menstruation imposes certain taboos on their public behavior and there is a conspicuous cultural difference between "little girls" and "maidens ripe for lovers." After puberty boys and girls are expected to enjoy sexual experiences, stopping short of full intercourse, before finally assuming marital responsibilities. Sexual morality is strictly defined as virginity, not chastity. Formerly, if an unmarried girl were found by her husband to have broken the law, her shame was indicated in a public ritual and the number of her marriage cattle was reduced. Today the ritual is discreetly modified, but there may still be a reduction in the number of her cattle, particularly if she has already born a child.

The period of relative sexual freedom is shorter for a girl, who is expected to marry a man several years her senior. The end of girlhood is marked by appropriate clothing and a change in hairstyle. A man should only marry when his age group receives permission from the king. Formerly, this was overtly symbolized by sewing on waxen headrings, but this was abandoned for the present king, whose grandmother, the Queen Regent Gwamile, considered it an unnecessary token of manhood for those who "put on hats" and had Western education. Very few headringed men survive, but marriage is still essential for the attainment of full tribal responsibilities and privileges. The married woman gains demonstrably in status with the birth of her first child, and reaches her highest position in the home of her married son. In old age, both men and women are entitled to veneration and care from the young; elders supervise the education of the young and lead the rituals.

Regimental Age Classes

Against these general age categories, individuals refer their own ages to important social episodes—wars, famines, epidemics, the arrival of important personalities, public celebrations—and, particularly in the case of men, to their age classes, or regiments (*emabutfo,* sing. *libutfo*).

The announcement of a new age class is made by the king when there is a representative gathering at the capital; it is the duty of those present at the gathering to inform others in their districts. The nucleus of the new group exists in the growing youths who already live in royal homesteads. A new age group should be formed every five to seven years when the last group is considered ready for marriage. The main dividing line between those groups permitted to marry and youths who may not yet "spill their strength in children" is drawn for purposes of ritual. When, in 1935, after a lapse of some fifteen years, Sobhuza II inaugurated the Locust Regiment at a public meeting, many in the "bachelor set" had already taken wives or given their lovers children. He later sent his messenger to collect a fine from these men for breaking the law, but the Christian Swazi, backed by missionaries, successfully objected to "interference" by a polygynous king in their private lives. This was one of the many situations in which the traditional political structure, sanctioned by ritual and ethics, conflicted with a new individualism and foreign religion.

Unlike other tribes in east and central Africa, the Swazi have no compulsory period of barrack life for every male. Each man is automatically recruited into a *libutfo*, but only a certain number reside more or less permanently in the public barracks attached to royal homesteads. These royal warriors (*emabutfo*) are distinguished from the rank and file (*emajaha*) who remain for the greater part of their lives in their own homesteads, or even in the homesteads of local chiefs, and who come to the royal centers only to perform specific services. *Emabutfo* have special titles, ornaments, songs and dances indicative of their higher status, and it is from this group that the king selects his most trusted messengers and attendants. Formerly men—especially if important—were eager that at least one of their sons should stay at state headquarters for some years, and family councils sent the heir to be educated in the etiquette and ways of the court. In addition to princes and sons of chiefs, poor commoners, who could derive few benefits from their own parents, offered their services to the rulers with the expectation that they would be suitably rewarded. The decision to become a "king's man" rests mainly with the individual; he need not obtain the prior consent of a father or guardian, for no one can prevent a subject from working for the king, the "father" of the nation. Thus, although every Swazi is automatically a member of an age class and there is no sharp distinction between civilian and soldier, the system makes a markedly different impact on individuals depending on whether or not they reside in a royal village.

Age classes are organized into distinctive units. The smallest is the squad (*siceme*) of eight to twenty men who stand together in the dance, an essential part of group activity, and form a recognized working team. Several squads join together to make a company (*licibia*), led by a prince, and each company has its own name, war cry, and decorations. The princes are subordinate to the regimental leader, or commander in chief—a commoner chosen by the king for his ability to maintain discipline, his military knowledge, trustworthiness, and loyalty. On national occasions he assumes control of all local contingents.

Age groups cut across the boundaries of local chiefs and across the bonds of kinship, incorporating individuals into the state, the widest political unit. Between members of the same regiment, and particularly those in permanent residence, there is a loyalty and camaraderie. They treat each other as equals, eat together, smoke hemp from the long hemp pipe that is part of their joint equipment, work together, and have a central meeting place or clubhouse in the barracks. They call each other "brother" or "my age mate," "my peer," and the ties between them are said to be stronger than those between kinsmen of different generations. Towards other age sets there is often openly expressed rivalry and occasional fights, usually provoked by disputes over beer or women, do occur. Young regiments resent the marital privileges of the older men who, in turn, attempt to keep the young from monopolizing as lovers girls old enough to become wives. To prevent feuds between the regiments national policy dictated periodic action against an external enemy.

Warfare was an essential function of the age classes, a clue to their former importance and present impotence. The Swazi, however, were never as aggressive as the Zulu in the period of military conquest, and though warfare offered the main opportunity for the display of individual courage and strength, Swazi leaders did not encourage reckless loss of life. When necessary, the regiments did not hesitate to retreat into their mountain caves; in battle formation the older regiments were strategically placed to control the younger and more foolhardy. The indoctrination of the army before it left for battle stressed both fierceness and cunning, and there were rituals for both national success and personal safety. Warriors who achieved a kill were decorated with medicated necklaces, and mimed their grand achievements in solo dancing at public gatherings. But they and their weapons were "cleansed of the blood" to prevent them from being infected with an obsessive urge to destroy.

Warfare was controlled so that it did not disrupt normal existence; the men usually left for battle only after they had completed the main work in the fields, and reserves always remained behind for economic and ritual duties. The regiments took no large quantity of food with them; they staved off hunger by smoking hemp and relied on obtaining meat from cattle looted from the enemy. During the warriors' absence, a strict supporting discipline was imposed on those who stayed behind. Wives and lovers in particular had to behave with special decorum, in the belief that if they were rowdy, drunk, or sexually "hot" they would subdue or "burn up" the strength of the warriors.

Death on the battlefield was considered a national sacrifice. Kinsmen were not allowed to mourn their dead who had fallen in battle and the king did not demand a beast for purification. Although warfare was extolled, the taking of life was considered fearful and dangerous. On its return, the army was "doctored" in a not always successful attempt to guard against the vengeful spirits of the dead. Warfare was considered an outlet for individual ambition and aggression but could not be allowed to become a menace to the peace of the state.

The last time the regiments functioned as traditional units was in the reign of Sobhuza's grandfather, but since then the Swazi have been indirectly involved in three major wars—the Anglo-Boer War, and the two world wars. In the Anglo-Boer War, the Swazi as a group remained neutral; in World War I, a small contingent served in France. In World War II, nearly 4000 were recruited by Sobhuza and sent to the Middle East where they built roads and fortifications, acted as stevedores, stretcher bearers, drivers, mechanics, and machine gunners. The whites have not, in practice, attacked militarism; they have not shown that fighting is bad, bloodshed in battle brutal, nor that nationalism is dangerous. They have increased rather than decreased the importance of armed strength as a source of national unity and individual security, but they have monopolized the power of force. Compared with the armaments of modern warfare, the traditional weapons (knives, spears, knobkerries, and shields) are antediluvian and the methods of using them have not even the superior strength of barbarism. A Westernized Swazi commented, "The whites have crushed intertribal war but they have introduced a false security of life and have stamped into Swazi culture the cheapness of individuals in an industrial economy."

Certain observances connected with warfare have been transferred to situations created by Western industry, especially deep-level mining. In conservative Swazi homes, women whose men work in the gold mines of South Africa follow the ritual precautions for protecting men engaged in battle; if a miner is killed in an underground accident his kinsmen do not have to pay death dues to the king. This transference of custom does not signify an identification of the value of death in the mines with that of death on the battlefield but an association of the two ways of dying through physical danger and attacks by hostile aliens.

The age sets were more precisely organized in the days of intertribal warfare than at present, but much of the structure survives for other than military purposes, which they continue to fulfill. When the regiments were not fighting they served as labor battalions, particularly for the aristocrats, and this remains one of their major duties. Their most intensive work depends on the agricultural routine of plowing, weeding, guarding the corn against the birds, reaping, and threshing; they may also be summoned to gather wood, cut leaves and poles for building, move huts, drive locusts off the fields, skin animals, run messages, fetch and carry. No matter how arduous a task may be, work begins and ends with the *blehla,* a dance song in the cattle pen. During the performance, which always attracts children and often the women of the homestead, individual workers dance out of the group and sing short songs of their own composition, boasting of some achievement or exhibiting their artistic virtuosity.

During their period in royal homesteads, warriors are responsible for their own subsistence, but the rulers are expected to provide them periodically with beer and meat. Formerly, when cattle were raided from hostile tribes the men were better fed; the present rulers are less able to support financially a large permanent retinue, and this is one of the main reasons for the decline in the numbers of *emabutfo.* Those who stay lead a precarious hand-to-mouth existence, relying largely on the generosity of the women in the neighborhood for whom they do occasional jobs, in their spare time, and wandering from beer drink to beer drink. Moreover, money has become a necessity since every male over the age of eighteen is required to pay an annual "poll tax," ranging from 35 shillings (roughly 5 dollars) for the unmarried to 90 shillings (roughly 13 dollars) for men with four or more wives. The king pays the tax for a few selected warriors, but most of the others are driven to work for whites; for the younger generation, the prestige derived from living at court is challenged by the opportunities and excitement of the new urban and industrial centers.

The age classes are, however, still required for state ritual, and at the annual ceremony of kingship, designed to rejuvenate the king and strengthen the people, separate duties are allocated to the oldest regiments, to the regiment of men in full vigor of manhood, and to the youths who are considered sexually pure. Ritual is part of the educative process, a symbolic affirmation of certain social values, and in traditional Swazi society where specialized formal educational institutions are nonexistent, the age classes serve as the main channels for inculcating the values of loyalty and group morality. The emphasis is less on the content of a curriculum, and the acquisition of new knowledge than on traditional values. In the past, special "old people" were appointed as instructors; teaching was not a separate career and learning was a gradual and continuous process of consolidation. The warriors are expected to master the main skills associated with adult life—in the barracks they even perform tasks normally left to women—and to develop the qualities of "manhood," specifically those related to the code of sexual morality. When a girl accepts a lover, she and her friends are expected to visit his barracks in special courting dress, which is brief but elaborately decorated with beads, and to sing and dance to make the relationship public. Should she on a subsequent visit find him absent, it is the duty of his agemates to try to see that she remains faithful to their friend. They find her accommodations and provide her with food. Lovers of other regiments are considered fair game, but the man who steals a girl of his own agemate is beaten and ostracized. In some other societies, sharing of women is a right of group membership; among the Swazi the emphasis on sexual monopoly over a particular lover is related to the ritual obligations placed on each member of an age group. In the main annual ceremony of the state, every individual of the unmarried regiment is responsible for contributing "pure strength" to kingship. At the present time, lover relationships are often not public and participation in state rituals is frequently evaded.

Education has, in fact, become secularized—to the extent that it has been taken from the control of the Swazi state with its particular framework of ritual and transferred to the education department of the Western administration. At the same time 90 percent of the schools in Swaziland are mission controlled, and mission institutions are by definition opposed to traditionalist values. The conflict between Christian churches and the Swazi state is producing a cleavage in the Swazi people between Christians and traditionalists, a cleavage that does not necessarily coincide with the division between the educated and uneducated. In 1936 Sobhuza attempted to bridge the gulf by suggesting the introduction of a modified age-class system in all the schools. The idea, investigated by anthropologists, met with the approval of the (unorthodox) head of the local administration, but the missionaries, who obviously could not support a system directed by a polygynous king, head of a tribal religion, offered the Pathfinder Movement (Black Boy Scouts) instead. Sobhuza's scheme was finally applied in three schools and maintained and financed by the Swazi nation itself. For various reasons, however, it failed to achieve a unity—which the Swazi state itself no longer represented. I mention this experiment in misguided "applied anthropology" because it illustrates these points: first, the awareness of tribal leaders of the conflict between traditionalist and Western values; second, the extent to which these values are deep rooted in social institutions such as chieftanship or church; third, the interaction of institutions in a wider power structure —the military nation as compared with a colonial government with limited authority over whites as well as Africans. The Swazi age-class system represents a passing social order. It grew with territorial expansion and the need to maintain political independence and internal security. Its weapons proved ineffectual against conquest, symbolized by monopolistic concessions, Western industry, counterreligious institutions, and a bureaucratic colonial system.

Swazi women are also organized into age sets of married and unmarried, but these are less formal than those of the men and do not extend under a common name throughout the nation. They are essentially local work teams that engage in specific tasks for district or national leaders. Women are never stationed in barracks, and the age of marriage for a girl is sanctioned by her parents and her friends, not by the rulers.

Sometimes a group of teen-agers are brought together under the patronage of unmarried princesses or daughters of chiefs into a temporary association, for which they lay down laws regulating clothing, food, language, and morality. No member may be "touched by a male," a regulation from which not even the king is immune. Violation of the code is punished by fines, imposed and collected by the girls, and also by organized songs of ridicule. The association, which begins and ends with tribute labor, lasts from one winter to the next, and the older girls are then publicly recognized as ripe for marriage.

In tribal society a person is a meeting point of identities—the identity of siblings, the identity of the lineage, the identity of the age group. The modern Western system gives greater scope to the individual, male or female, young and old. When conflict breaks out in conservative homesteads between parent and child generations or between older and younger siblings, it is not a conflict of ideologies but of personality. Sons may covet the power of the father, but when he dies, they hope to exercise over their own sons the authority they themselves once resented. Young people are anxious to possess the privileges of their seniors, not to abolish the privileges of seniority; young brides may rebel against the way particular in-laws abuse the rights of age, but they agree to the principle that age and sex are entitled to those rights. At the present time, the social structure which gives power to the older generation is challenged by the money economy, a new legal system, and schooling for a literate society. A son is still dependent on his father and ultimately on his chief for the land on which to build his home, but he is legally permitted to move for working purposes into the European town and support himself on money wages. The manual occupations opened by Western enterprise require physical strength, for which the old are rejected, while the young and fit are in demand and able to contract in terms of their personal legal status. Formal education weakens the claim of the uneducated that the possession of the greatest knowledge is obtainable only through age. Books and classes, quick roads to learning, contradict the system of gradual education in which the major phases of physical development are correlated with responsibilities associated with the group of peers.

6

The Supernatural

The Spirit World

SWAZI CULTURE sanctions enjoyment of the material and physical: food, women, and dancing. It does not in any way idealize poverty or place a value on suffering as a means to happiness or salvation. To deal with the hazards of life—failure of crops, unfaithfulness of women, illness and ultimate death—the culture provides a set of optimistic notions and positive stereotyped techniques that are especially expressed through the ancestral cult, the vital religion of the Swazi, and through an elaborate system of magic. The ancestors sanction the desires of their descendants; magic provides the techniques for the achievement of these desires.

In the ancestral cult, the world of the living is projected into a world of spirits (*emadloti*). Men and women, old and young, aristocrats and commoners, continue the patterns of superiority and inferiority established by earthly experiences. Paternal and maternal spirits exercise complementary roles similar to those operating in daily life on earth; the paternal role reinforces legal and economic obligations; the maternal exercises a less formalized protective influence. Although the cult is set in a kinship framework, it is extended to the nation through the king, who is regarded as the father of all Swazi; his ancestors are the most powerful of the spirits.

Swazi believe that the spirit or breath has an existence distinct from the flesh. When a person dies, both flesh and spirit must be correctly treated to safeguard the living. Mortuary ritual varies with both the status of the deceased and his (or her) relationship with different categories of mourners. The more important the dead, the more elaborate the rites given the corpse; the closer the relationship through blood or marriage, the greater the stereotyped interest demanded by the spirit of the mourners. A headman is buried at the entrance of the cattle byre, and his widows, children, siblings, and other relatives are constrained to undertake different demonstrations and periods of mourning.

The widows shave their heads and remain "in darkness" for three years before they are given the duty of continuing the lineage of the deceased through the levirate. A wife is more expendable; the deceased woman is buried on the outskirts of her husband's home, and the mourning imposed on him is less conspicuous, less rigorous, and of shorter duration. The social order regulates overt demonstrations of grief, irrespective of the depth of personal emotions. Death, more than any other situation in Swazi culture, exposes the *social* personality of man, woman, and child in the fullest context of kinship. The living must, in turn, adjust to the loss by building new bonds on established structural foundations.

The spirit of the deceased is ritually "brought back" to the family in a feast that ends all active mourning; the spirit continues, however, to influence the destinies of kinsmen. It may manifest itself in illness and in various omens, or it may materalize in the form of a snake. Mambas are associated with kings; harmless green snakes are associated with commoners and women; and certain snakes are excluded from the ancestral realm because they '"never come nicely." An ancestral snake does not show fear and moves with familiar sureness within the hut. It is a bad omen if such a snake comes in and quickly leaves. The body of every Swazi is believed to have at least one snake, which is associated with fertility and health. It is somehow connected with the spiritual snake, but is not conceptualized in any elaborate theory of transmigration or reincarnation. The existence of an ancestral snake is simply stated as fact, with the emphasis on practical implications.

Illness and other misfortunes are frequently attributed to the ancestors, but Swazi believe that *emadloti* do not inflict sufferings through malice or wanton cruelty. The mean husband, the adulterous wife, the overambitious younger brother, the disobedient son may be dealt with directly or vicariously by the spirits, acting as custodians of correct behavior and tribal ethics. Ancestors punish, they do not kill; death is the act of evildoers (*batsakatsi*), who are interested in destroying, not in perpetuating, the lineage or the state. If an illness originally divined as sent by the *emadloti* later becomes fatal, evildoers are assumed to have taken advantage of the patient's weak resistance.

While each specific death is interpreted as an act of witchcraft, death is also recognized as universal and inevitable. In a myth, widespread throughout the southeastern tribes, death was imposed by the arbitrary and inconsistent nature of the "Great Great One," "The First Being," a vaguely conceived "Great Ancestor." He sent the chameleon to mankind with a message of eternal life, then changed His mind and sent the lizard with the message of death. To the African, the chameleon, with its peculiar mottled and changing skin color and its markedly protruding eyes that turn in all directions is quite distinct from the ordinary lizard, which glides along without changing color and has sleepy eyes that look only straight ahead. The lizard arrived before the chameleon, who had stopped to eat of tasty berries growing by the wayside. When the chameleon arrived and delivered his message, he was driven away—death had already become part of life. The Great Great One apparently did not again intervene in the affairs of men, and no prayers or ritual are associated with Him. Many Christian missionaries use the vernacular word for Great Great One as a translation of the Biblical God, but the ideas underlying the two deities are worlds apart.

Ancestors have greater wisdom, foresight, and power than the rest of mankind, but no spirit of a deceased ever reaches complete deification or is regarded as omnipotent. Swazi ancestors are approached as practical beings; there is no conflict between the ethics of the ancestral cult and the mundane desires of life. Swazi desire the ends they say the *emadloti* desire for them. Swazi are not concerned with the life led by the dead, but with the way the ancestors influence their lives on earth. No one inquires from a diviner if the *emadloti* are happy and satisfied, till they show they are unhappy and dissatisfied. Ancestral spirits, like witches and sorcerers, are thought of most when comforts are few and troubles are many.

Swazi have no class of ordained priests, and the privileged duty of appealing to the *emadloti* rests with the head of the family. The father acts on behalf of his sons; if he is dead, the older brother acts on behalf of the younger. In this patrilineal society, ancestors of a married woman remain at her natal home; they are approachable only by her senior male kinsman, but they retain a protective interest in the woman who has provided cattle through her marriage, and in her children who consolidated her position as a wife. Contact is usually made through the medium of food, meat, or beer, and the dead, who are said to be often hungry, "lick" the essence of the offerings laid at dusk on a sacred place in the shrine hut and left overnight. The family head addresses the dead in much the same way as if they were alive; appeals to them are spontaneous and conversational, interspersed with rebukes and generally devoid of gratitude. Recognition of the holy, as distinct from the profane, is, moreover, expressed on certain occasions through sacred songs. Each clan has a special song and there are a number of anthems reserved for rituals of state.

Each family propitiates its own ancestors at the specific domestic events of birth, marriage, death, and the building and moving of huts; in addition, the royal ancestors periodically receive public recognition. Every year before the rains are due cattle are sent from the capital to the caves in two tree-covered groves, where dead kings and leading princes lie buried in order of seniority. The groves, described as frightening and awe inspiring, alive with the sound of majestic voices and the movement of great snakes, are in the charge of important chiefs in the vicinity. They must see that no one enters without permission, and there is a current mythology concerning the doom of unfortunates who unwittingly intruded into the domain of the sacred. The ruler's emissaries report the affairs of the country to the dead and appeal for prosperity, health, and rain. Some of the cattle are sacrificed; the others are brought back to the royal village, where various taboos have been imposed on normal behavior. The cattle are brought in on a night when the moon is full, and the ordinary people are ordered to wait in their huts in silence while the king and his mother meet the returning pilgrims. Together they walk through the great cattle pen chanting a sacred song associated with major developments of kingship. That night the gates are left open, so that the ancestral cattle may wander freely through the village. The following day, there is the main sacrifice, in which each animal is dedicated to specific dead and eaten in a sacramental feast. So close is the identification between the animal and the human, that kinsmen who would have practiced avoidance of the person in life are prohibited from eating of the flesh of the sacrificial victim.

Subordinate to the ancestral cult, suggesting a separate cultural influence—another layer of tradition—is the recognition accorded the forces of nature. The sun, moon, and rainbow are personified, and though they are not appealed to directly, they are drawn into the orbit of human destiny. Swazi believe that the earth is flat and that the sun, the male, crosses the sky in a regular path twice a year. Each night he sleeps and wakens again strong and refreshed. The moon is the woman who dies periodically and is connected with the cycle of fertility. The rainbow is the sign of the "Princess of the Sky," associated with spring. All major rituals are timed by the position of the sun and moon. Ancestral spirits are most active at dawn and dusk, and ceremonies to mark an increase in status are generally performed when the moon is waxing or full; ceremonies that temporarily isolate a man from his fellows take place when it is waning, or "in darkness."

As previously stated, rain is in a different category from most other natural phenomena. It is believed to be controlled by medicines associated with kingship and is interpreted as a sign of ancestral blessing and good will. Knowledge of rainmaking is secret to the queen mother, her son and three trusted assistants, but every subject is aware that at certain times the rulers are "working the rain." The techniques they use increase in strength with the month and general climatic conditions, and move, if necessary, over a period of time from minor to more elaborate rites. Failure to make rain come has many explanations: disobedience and disloyalty of the people; breach of taboos; hostility between the rulers themselves, and other actions that evoke the prohibitive anger of the royal ancestors. The efficacy of the medicines is not doubted—rain eventually falls—and the belief in the rulers as rainmakers, a belief held even by many Christians, remains one of the strongest sanctions of traditional Swazi power. Lightning, on the other hand, is associated with the "Bird of the Sky," which lives in certain pools and can be controlled by particularly powerful evildoers. There are special lightning doctors to treat homesteads and people with antilightning medicines.

A rich body of folklore relates various places, plants, and animals to the world of men, but the Swazi have no store of sacred oral literature. The world of nature is of much the same order and quality as the world of man, and the animal kingdom in particular provides characters and situations that illustrate the aspirations, contradictions, and conflicts experienced by humans. No special tales based on the ancestral world or nature are accredited to divine inspiration. In the hierarchically structured but kinship-oriented society of the Swazi, articulate revelation is restricted to medicine and divination.

Specialists in Ritual

In all situations requiring "deep" (esoteric) knowledge, Swazi consult medicine men (*tinyanga temitsi*) and/or their colleagues, the diviners (*tangoma*), the main specialists in Swazi traditional society. Medicine men work primarily with "trees" (roots, bark, leaves) and other natural substances, and enter the profession of their own accord; diviners diagnose the cause rather than direct the specific cure and rely on spirit possession for their insight. Within the two major categories of ritual specialists several grades are distinguished on the basis of training and technique.

Every Swazi has some knowledge of "medicines" for common ailments and other misfortunes (poor crops, failure in love, sick cattle) and the lowest grade of ritual specialist includes people who, usually through personal experience, have picked up remedies for specific purposes and are not prepared to disclose their secrets without reward. They claim no inspiration from the ancestors and no tradition of belonging to a family of doctors. Behind their backs they are spoken of contemptuously as "crocodiles,"—the quacks—and they are said to be increasing in number since they have had the opportunity of acquiring medicines from men outside the country and from Western drugstores. Informants say that some of these self-taught specialists are skillful enough but insist that the ancestors must subsequently have agreed that their work meets with success.

More highly rated are the medicine men whose careers are destined from birth or sanctioned by the powerful dead. Knowledge of rituals and medicine bags are retained in certain families as an important part of the inheritance. The owner imparts them to a favorite son, a younger brother, or close kinsman, who is "pushed by the heart to learn" and need not be the main heir. Once qualified, he calls on the "father spirit" in each situation and periodically renews the power of the bags in ritual reaffirmation of his spiritual dependence.

Some *tinyanga* specialize very intensively and will treat only a single illness or misfortune; others have a very diversified practice and offer panaceas for an extensive and varied range of difficulties. Added tension and insecurity have multiplied the situations for which medicines are desired, and many illiterate Swazi apply the same principiles to get better jobs, make profitable beer sales, or "sweeten the mouths" of men brought before magistrates for breaking the "white man's laws." Specialists in ritual, unlike specialists in handicrafts, effectively resisted change, and while many mundane objects were easily replaced by trade goods, the range of "medicines" has been extended.

In Swazi "medicine" the material ingredients are emphasized more than the verbal spell. These ingredients are frequently chosen on the familiar principles of homeopathic magic—like produces like, and things once in contact retain identity even when separated by distance. Their names may indicate the purpose of the rite for which they are used and serve as abbreviated spells. Thus, in a love potion of a leading *inyanga*, the main ingredient is a resilient, everlasting leaf named "disobey her mother"; for the medicine to secure a homestead against evildoers, "pegs" are cut from a tree that remains firm in the thinnest soil on a precarious slope. In the treatment for success, instructions given by an *inyanga* must be implicitly obeyed and any pain he inflicts must be stoically endured. Most doctoring for even indirect benefits (household safety, protection against lightning, as well as personal quandaries—love, ill health) involve techniques such as injections, inhalation, and purgatives. In all but intimate sexual affairs, all people in the homestead must take part, for each member is recognized as interacting with others, and correct adjustment of social relationships is considered essential for a successful result.

The Swazi have no association of medicine men. Each *inyanga* works alone, drawing on a common stock of traditionally "proven" remedies to which he may add his own findings. Each *inyanga* is conspicuous by his "bags"— pouches, calabashes, and charms—and when consulted he proudly displays their contents and expatiates on their "strength." Success is also attributed to the innate "power" (personality?) of the practitioner, whose own life conditions should support his professional claims. Renowned medicine men are themselves men of substance, and the profession provides the main opportunity for the individualist of traditional society.

The diviners, often people of outstanding intelligence, are the most powerful and respected of specialists. Their nonconformity is sanctioned by the spirits. The first sympton of possession is usually an illness that is difficult to cure and frequently follows terrible physical or emotional experiences. The patient becomes fastidious about food, eats little, complains of pains in various parts of the body and strange sensations between his shoulder blades and in his head. After sacrifices and medicines have proved useless, an already established diviner may diagnose that the sufferer is troubled by a spirit that must be made to express itself. Inarticulate noises and wild behavior indicate possession by the wandering ghost of a stranger or of an animal, and treatment is directed to its expulsion, or exorcism, by "closing its road." On the other hand, possession by friendly humans, most frequently kinsmen, is considered socially beneficial and the patient is encouraged to become a diviner. This involves long and arduous training during which he wanders over the countryside, eats little, sleeps little, is tormented by fearful dreams—of snakes encircling his limbs, of drowning in a flooded river, of being torn to pieces by enemies: he becomes "a house of dreams." These dreams must be interpreted to forestall misfortune to himself and others. He is also purified with special potions and various medicines to enable him to hear and see the spirit that is guiding him. Each novice composes a song and when he sings it, villagers come and join in the chorus to help him develop his powers.

A master diviner may have several novices living at his home for varying periods, forming an embryonic ritual school. When he considers them to be fully trained he puts them through a public graduation ceremony. Spectators hide articles for them to discover and they are also expected to throw hints to selected members of the audience about their various predicaments. As in many transition rites, each novice is said to be "reborn" and is honored with gifts of goats, special clothing, and beads to mark the change in status.

Despite the prestige and power of diviners most people do not wish to become possessed. The reasons given express socially inculcated attitudes to this type of greatness. It is best to be normal, not to be limited all one's life by the special taboos on sex, food, and general behavior that are imposed by the profession, not to be exhausted by the demands of a spirit greater than oneself, not to have to shoulder responsibility for the life and death of others. There are men therefore, who try to stop the spirit even in cases of ancestral possession, but on the whole such tampering is considered dangerous since it may leave a person permanently delicate and deranged, an object of spite by the spirit he has thrust from him and of neglect by others, angered at the reception given to one of their kind.

Although very few Swazi women practice as herbalists, more women than men appear to be "possessed," and there are a large number of well-known women diviners. The difference in number of women herbalists and diviners is a consequence of the sexual division of labor and the relative statuses of male and female. A woman's duty is the care of home and children. An herbalist who must wander around the countryside to dig roots and collect plants is brought into intimate contact with strangers, and this is contrary to the norm laid down for female behavior. As a result, girls are rarely taught medicines by their fathers, the heir to the family bags is always male, and no husband encourages a woman to practice medicine. Possession, however, is in a different category. A woman does not fight against the spirit of an ancestor that wishes to "turn her around," and even her husband is afraid to interfere and must submit to her "calling."

Political leaders and other aristocrats are positively discouraged from becoming either medicine men or diviners, for this would interfere with their administrative duties and does not fit into their ascribed status. At the same time, they employ *tinyanga* of all types to bolster their powers, and the *ingwenyama* is himself believed to have "deeper" knowledge of medicines than any of his subjects and to be able to detect evildoers without preliminary possession by virtue of his unique royal medicines.

In most séances the clients sit in a semicircle on the ground, chant songs, and clap their hands while the diviner, in full regalia, smokes *dagga*** and dances himself into a high pitch of excitement. He asks no questions but makes statements to which the audience replies, "We agree." Each statement is a feeler, a clue whereby he builds up his case, piecing together the evidence from the emotion behind the responses, until finally he gives the desired information. Diviners, often shrewd judges of human nature, have a wide knowledge of local affairs and their interpretations generally, perhaps unconsciously, confirm the suspicions or crystallize the unspoken fears of their clients. It is however, often considered desirable to consult other diviners who may use dif-

---

* *Dagga* is a potent drug, similar to marihuana.

ferent methods. An increasing number of modern diviners "throw bones," a technique associated with Sotho and Tonga influence. The "bones" may be the astragali of goats, cowrie shells found on the East Coast, or oddly shaped seeds. The diviner, pointing to the different pieces, interprets the combination of positions. Exceptional divinatory devices include the "talking calabash" (a ventriloquist trick), a rattle that shakes of its own accord, and a magic wand. Public séances to "smell out evildoers" are prohibited under the Witchcraft Ordinance, but continue secretly in the frontier regions. In Namahasha, high in the Lebombo between Portuguese and Swazi territory, I have seen a diviner in full regalia, "smelling out" with a magically impregnated hippo whip as he danced in front of a tense audience that had come from a homestead some fifty miles away to learn the "cause" of a sequence of misfortunes and deaths. The poison "ordeal" may be administered as the ultimate test: the innocent will not be affected, but the guilty will writhe, vomit, and confess. The poison is collected in Portuguese territory; as a rule, diviners from that area are asked to assist in its preparation, but its use must be sanctioned by the *ingwenyama.*

Over the years new techniques of divination have been introduced and integrated with traditional modes of thought and behavior. Allied to the traditional diviner are "prophets" who belong to certain Separatist churches and claim to be possessed by the Holy Ghost, in which guise they carry on both divination and exorcism with less fear of "white man's law." There have also been two associations, similar to those in other parts of Africa, that have been directed against witchcraft in general, and have reaffirmed the strength of divination.

Witchcraft

Medicine men and diviners, official supporters of law and authority, have as their illegal opposition the evildoers (*batsakatsi*). Swazi *batsakatsi* include witches, whose evil is both physiological and psychological, and sorcerers, who rely on poisons, conscious violence, or other techniques for the deliberate destruction of property or person. The propensity to witchcraft is transmitted through a woman to her children, male and female; a male does not pass it on to his offspring. The initial quality must, however, be further developed by injections and training, or the potential witch will be mischievous but ineffectual. Qualified witches are believed to form a permanent gang, within which they are ranked on the basis of evil achievements. They operate at night; during the day they gloat consciously on their nefarious activities. A sorcerer obtains his "poisons" from outside and acts individually in specific situations against personal enemies. To be effective he may seek assistance from a medicine man who, by collusion, also becomes an evildoer; the most powerful *tinyanga* are therefore sometimes feared as the greatest *batsakatsi.*

Batsakatsi may work through direct contact with the person by striking a victim through his food. The reality of the power of evildoers is considered self-evident; it is manifest in otherwise inexplicable misfortunes and confirmed by confessions at séances and ordeals. Moreover, at the end of every individual's life, sorcery or witchcraft turns up the trump card of death.

Murders for "doctoring" (so-called ritual murders) still take place in Swaziland, and fall into two main situational types: (1) agricultural fertility; (2) personal aggrandisement. The victim, referred to as "a buck," is innocent of any crime and is killed with as much secrecy as possible. An analysis of the European court records indicated that the characteristics of sex, age, and pigmentation of the victims showed no uniformity, and that different organs were selected from the corpse. Where the accused were found guilty of murdering for "medicine" to doctor the crops, capital punishment was carried out on the principals; others involved were sentenced to imprisonment with hard labor for periods ranging from fifteen years to life; in murders for personal aggrandisement the death penalty was invariably imposed, but in certain circumstances it was commuted to a long term of imprisonment. The men employing the "doctors" were generally important headmen, sometimes chiefs suffering economic or status insecurity. The average Swazi condemns murders committed in self-interest as sorcery, and places the ritual specialist who gave the instructions in a different moral and legal category from the diviner who, in his capacity as a witchfinder, may be responsible for the destruction of people publicly revealed as evildoers. The distinction is not accepted by Western law.

Swazi complain that *batsakatsi* are more common now than in the past and blame the law that has made "smelling out" by diviners illegal. They argue that "the white man's law protects women and witches. Bad men flourish and those who smell them out are hanged." But, in fact, any increase in sorcery, as in other types of magic, must be sought in additional situations of conflict, feelings of inadequacy and helplessness, financial uncertainty, rivalry for jobs, competition for the favor of white employers, and personal insecurity in an alien-dominated milieu.

Witchcraft and sorcery can be directed against anyone, but because they emanate from hatred, fear, jealousy and thwarted ambition they are usually aimed at persons who are already connected by social bonds. The social content is stereotyped by the alignments of Swazi society and indicates points of tension or friction, actual or anticipated. In the polygynous homestead, the *umstakatsi* is usually a jealous co-wife or an unscrupulous half brother who is ambitious of the inheritance; outside the homestead, suspected evildoers are blatantly successful and aggressive peers. Important men do not need to use sorcery against insignificant inferiors, nor are they suspected of doing so. Sorcery is an indication of status and of the ambitions for improvement of status that operate within the limits of the stratified traditional society. Thus, not all destructive ritual is condemned as the work of evildoers, nor do all "productive" medicines receive social approval. Judgment depends on the situation. It is legitimate to use retaliative medicine on the grave of a person whose death was attributed to an unidentified evildoer, or to doctor property so that a thief will be inflicted with swollen finger joints, or to inject into an unfaithful wife medicine that will punish her lover with a wasting disease. It is illicit to employ productive medicine for unlimited wealth or success. In short, the *umstakatsi* undermines the *status quo;* the *inyanga* struggles to maintain it. Wedged between the chief and the *tinyanga* on the one hand and the *batsakatsi* on the other, the masses are molded to accept a relatively unenterprising conservatism.

Christianity

Traditional Swazi religion is challenged by Christianity. In 1946 nearly 40 percent of Swazi were registered as "Christians" and more than twenty different sects were listed. In Swaziland, as in the Republic of South Africa, a growing number of converts belong to Independent or "Separatist churches," which vary greatly in organization and credo but share one common characteristic —independence from white control. These churches offer new opportunities for self-expression and power; many of the founders are men of unusual personality, and some are more highly educated than the average Swazi.

Largely because of tribal status and a vested interest in polygyny, Swazi male aristocrats have tended to resist conversion from the ancestral cult, but their mothers and wives have been more responsive. The Methodists were the first to establish a mission in Swaziland. The late Indlovukati Lomawa was a recognized supporter of the church, though the National Council ruled that full conversion—including the clothing in which it could be demonstrated— was incompatible with the ritual duties of her position. She was particularly sympathetic to the Zionist Separatist church, whose charismatic local leader had converted close members of her natal family, and, at the same time, had acknowledged the claims of hereditary kingship exercised by her son, the *Ingwenyama.* When she died, she was buried according to custom away from the capital in a former royal village, so that her son would not be weakened by contact with death or the dead. At her funeral—which her son was not permitted to attend— various church officials paid their respects. Despite the fact that leading councilors tried to follow traditional practices, the entire mortuary procedure was interrupted for a few hours when her sister, who later succeeded to the position of queen mother, found that the church membership cards of the deceased (described as her "tickets across the Jordan") had been left behind at the capital. These were fetched and placed beside the dead woman in a wooden coffin that had been specially shaped to hold her body which was bound in fetal position and wrapped in a shroud of black cowhide.

The traditional religion has been influenced by Christianity, and Christianity as practiced by the Swazi has, in turn, been influenced by existing traditions. The extent of adaptation by the white-controlled churches ranges from the eclectic approach of Catholics to the rigidity of extreme Afrikaner Calvinists.* The Catholic church, which began work in 1914, later than most churches in

---

* Afrikaner is the term for white South Africans who speak Afrikaans, a local language developed mainly from Dutch. Afrikaners tend to be culturally insular, and strongly racialist.

Swaziland, increased its enrollment more rapidly than any other white-controlled church. But the proselytizing influence of all white missions virtually came to a standstill in the late 1930s, when the nativistic African Separatist movement boomed on an upsurge of nationalism. Separatist "Zionist" leaders consulted with Sobhuza and decided to form the Swazi National Church, with a flexible dogma and great tolerance of custom. Sobhuza was thus to be ritually entrenched, both as head of the traditional ancestral cult and as priest-king of a new faith, a position different from that in neighboring areas where traditional chieftanship had been deliberately broken down or where the chief himself had been converted to Christianity. At the same time, separatist movements cannot—by definition—really create lasting unity. A church, planned as a memorial to the late Lomawa and designed by an imaginative European architect, was half-built when friction, accentuated by lack of funds, broke out between the leaders and construction stopped. So the walls remain roofless, symbolizing a religious and secular unity that is desired but does not exist in modern Swaziland.

The Annual Ceremony of Kingship

Throughout this study I have mentioned the annual ritual of kingship, the *Incwala,* a ceremony rich in Swazi symbolism and only understandable in terms of the social organization and major values of Swazi life. It has been variously interpreted as a first-fruit ceremony, a pageant of Swazi history, a drama of kingship, and a ritual of rebellion. This beautiful and complex ceremony is described and analyzed in great detail in *An African Aristocracy;* here, I can but outline some of the main sequences and characteristics.

The central figure is the king, the "owner" of the *Incwala;* performance of the *Incwala* by anyone else is treason, which, on two historic occasions, cost the lives of overambitious princes. The *Incwala* reflects the growth of the king and is thus not a static ritual. When the king is a minor, the ritual is less elaborate, the medicines less potent, the animals required for doctoring smaller, the clothing simpler. When he reaches full manhood and has his first ritual wife, the *Incwala* reaches its peak. All subjects play parts determined by their status: the queen mother, the queens, married and unmarried regiments, princes, the king's artificial blood brothers, councilors, ordinary commoners, and ritual specialists known as "People of the Sea," all have specific duties and receive appropriate treatment.

The *Incwala* is a sacred period set apart from the profane and mundane routine of normal life. It extends for roughly three weeks of each year, and is divided into the Little *Incwala,* which lasts two days, beginning when the sun reaches its southern summer solstice and the moon is dark, and the Big *Incwala,* which lasts six days from the night of the full moon. In the interim period, sacred songs and dances of the Little *Incwala* are performed in key villages throughout the territory. It is believed that wrong timing will bring national disaster that can only be circumvented by elaborate counter-ritual, a common cultural device to make people abide by tradition, yet not automatically accept calamity.

The *Incwala* involves considerable organization and preparation. Several weeks before the ceremony the "People of the Sea" are brought to the capital for initial arrangements, and are then sent out to collect the water and other ritual ingredients. They divide into two groups, one travelling through the forests to the coast and the other to the confluence of the main rivers of the country. They must draw "the waters of all the world" and also dig potent sacred plants to strengthen and purify the king. In every homestead where the priests rest, the host provides beer and meat, and from all strangers who cross their paths they demand a small fine, which will be burnt on the last day, the day of final national purification. At the capital itself, preparations are made by the councilors, who will also be held responsible for the correct timing.

The honor of opening the *Incwala* is bestowed on the oldest regiment. Thereafter, other participants join in, taking their places according to rank and sex. The stage is the open cattle pen of the capital, but the main rites are enacted in secret in the king's sanctuary. The public contributes by performing sacred songs and dances. As the sun sets in a moonless night, the formation of the dances changes from the crescent of a new moon to the circle of the full moon. Princes and foreigners are dismissed as the warriors chant a new song that is associated with other important events of kingship—a king's marriage to his main ritual wife, the return of ancestral cattle from the royal grave, the burial of kings. It is a key song of the *Incwala*.

> Jjiya oh o o King, alas for your fate
> Jjiya oh o o King, they reject thee
> Jjiya oh o o King, they hate thee.

Suddenly the chief councilor commands "Silence," and the singing ceases while the king spits powerful medicine, first to the east, then to the west, and the crowd is given the signal to shout, "He stabs it!" Informants explained that "Our Bull (Our King) had produced the desired effect: he had triumphed and was strengthening the earth." He has broken off the old year and is preparing for the new." This climaxes the opening of the ceremony. The people then sing a final song comparable to a national anthem, praising the king as "the Bull, the Lion, the Inexplicable, the Great Mountain." At dawn of the following day, the ceremony is repeated. Afterwards, warriors go to weed the queen mother's garden, for which service they are rewarded with a feast of meat. The Little *Incwala* is over, and the men may return to their homes until the moon is "ripe."

In royal homesteads, the songs and dances of the Little *Incwala* are rehearsed and the sacred costumes are prepared for the main ceremony. The words of the songs are surprising to Europeans, who are accustomed to hear royalty blatantly extolled, the virtues of the nation magnified, and the country glorified at national celebrations. Most songs of the *Incwala* have as their motif hatred of the king, and his rejection by the people. The actual words are few, mournful, and tremendously moving; they are reinforced by dancing, which mimes much of the drama. The beautiful clothing, including feathers of special birds and skins of wild animals, indicates differences in rank and also carrys deep magical and religious significance.

On the first day of the Big *Incwala,* the regiment of pure unmarried youths is sent to cut branches of a magic tree with which to enclose the king's sanctuary. Swazi believe that if the branches are cut by anyone who has violated the moral code of his age group, the leaves will wither. Such branches must be cast out and the culprit ostracized and even attacked, not so much for his sexual violations as for his willingness to endanger the well-being of the state. The tree is quick-growing, with leaves that remain green for many weeks, when cut by the virtuous. The cutting must begin as the full moon rises, to the rhythm of a new sacred song—a sacred lullaby—the theme song of the second stage of the drama. The qualities of quick growth, greenness, toughness, and fertility characterize most elements of the *Incwala* ritual.

On the morning of the second day, the youths return, bearing their wands proudly aloft and chanting the lullaby. The councilors surround the sanctuary with the mystic greenery, behind which the powers of the king will be symbolically reborn.

The main event of the third day is the "killing of the bull," the symbol of potency. The king strikes a specially selected black bull with a rod doctored for fertility and "awakening," and the pure youths must catch the animal, throw it to the ground, pummel it with their bare hands, and drag it into the sanctuary where it is sacrificed. Parts of the carcass are used for royal medicine; the remainder is an offering to the ancestors.

The "Day of the Bull" fortifies the king for the "Great Day" when he appears in his most terrifying image and symbolically overcomes the hostility of princely rivals. In the morning he bites "doctored" green foods of the new year; his mother and others follow suit, their medicines graded by status. Later in the day, under the blazing sun, all the people, in full *Incwala* dress, and with the king in their midst, dance and sing the *Incwala*. Towards sunset the king leaves them; when he re-emerges he is unrecognizable—a mythical creature—clothed in a fantastic costume of sharp-edged green grass and skins of powerful wild animals, his body gleaming with black unguents. The princes approach and alternately drive him from them into the sanctuary and beseech him to return. Behind them the people sing and dance. All members of the royal Dlamini clan and all "foreigners" (seen as potential enemies) are ordered from the cattle byre; the king remains and dances with his loyal supporters and common subjects. Tension mounts as he sways backwards and forwards. At the climax he appears holding in his hand a vivid-green gourd, known as the "Gourd of Embo" (the north), the place of Dlamini origin. Although picked the previous year, the gourd is still green. The king throws it lightly on the horizontally placed shield of a selected agemate, who must not let the fruit, sacred vessel of the past and symbol of continuity, touch the ground. The old year has been discarded; the king has proved his strength, and the people are prepared for the future.

Life does not immediately return to its normal routine; major rites of transition generally involve gradual readjustments. The whole of the following day the rulers are secluded and unapproachable, their faces painted dark with medicines, their bodies anointed with fat from the sacred herd. Subjects are placed in a condition of ritual identification and prohibited from many normal physical activities—sex, washing, scratching, merrymaking. There is a deep silence at the capital. The *Incwala* songs are closed for the year.

On the last day, the ointments of darkness are washed off the rulers, who are then bathed with foamy potions to make them "shine" anew. Objects used throughout the ceremony, and which represent the old year, are burned on a ritual fire. The king sets light to the wood (which must be without thorns) with ancient fire sticks and walks naked and alone round the pyre, sprinkling medicated waters. At noon, he and his people, dressed in partial *Incwala* clothing, gather in the cattle pen for the final scene. They perform a series of solemn, but not sacred, dance-songs; rain—the blessing of the ancestors—must fall, quenching the flames and drenching all the participants. If no rain falls, the people fear a year of dire misfortune. But the rains usually come, and in the evening the rulers provide vast quantities of meat and beer, and there is gaiety and love-making. Early the next morning the warriors collect in the cattle byre, sing ordinary march songs, and go to weed the queen mother's largest maize garden. The local contingents are then free to return to their homes, where they may safely eat of the crops of the new season.

Now for some brief comments on certain general features of the *Incwala*. Culturally, it is a dramatic ritualization of Swazi kingship in all its complexity—economic, military, ritual. The sacrament of the first fruits, an essential rite in a series of rites, relates the rulers to the productive cycle, and the timing links them mystically with the great powers of nature—the sun and the moon. Fertility and potency are stressed as essential qualities of social continuity and must be acquired by stereotyped techniques. Swazi (like all people) believe that the efficacy of ritual lies in correct repetition; certain changes have been made in the course of time but the tendency has been to add new items rather than discard old.

The *Incwala* symbolizes the unity of the state and attempts to maintain it. Fighting and bloodshed are recognized as possible dangers at a time when regiments from all parts of the country are mobilized at the capital. The men are prohibited from carrying spears and *assegais,* the main weapons of attack; only shields and sticks are incorporated in the costume. Emotional fervor is canalized in songs, and dances, obligatory acts of participation that induce the sacred pulse, the *tactus* of Swazi national life. Internal solidarity is frequently intensified by outside opposition; the king outshines his rivals and the nation is fortified against external enemies. In the past, the *Incwala* frequently preceded an announcement of war against a "foreign tribe."

The people committed to the *Incwala* represent the social groups that accept the authority of the traditional rulers; those who deliberately refrain from taking part indicate the limitations of their present acceptance. Certain missions prohibited their converts from dancing the *Incwala,* and those Swazi Christians who attend are mainly members of Separatist churches. It is significant that, since 1937, the leader of the main Zionist Separatist sect has travelled to the capital for the *Incwala,* thereby publicly demonstrating his support of Swazi kingship. Thus the *Incwala* serves as a graph of status on which the roles of the king, his mother, the princes, councilors, priests, princesses, commoners, old and young are mapped by ritual. The balance of power between the king and the princes and between the aristocrats and commoners is a central theme; the ambivalent position of a Swazi king and the final triumph and sanctity of kingship is dramatized in ritual. The groups and individuals who have no set roles in the present-day *Incwala* reflect the influence of European dominance and of a new basis of stratification.

7

Continuity in Change

I T HAS BECOME platitudinous to state that Africa in the past decade has
been swept by the "winds of change." Since the independence of Ghana
in 1957, thirty-three former African colonies have been admitted to the
United Nations, and even more remote areas of Africa have become foci of international interest. The details of change in the different areas and the reaction
to the new developments are, however, complex and varied. In this final chapter
I shall briefly indicate a few major trends in Swaziland. Social change generally
involves selection, and deliberate selection is always influenced by past experience. Some traditional customs and institutions adjust readily, others show a
tenacity or resistance that is often difficult to explain in terms of Western
motivation or rationale. But the process of integrating the new with the old
cannot be locally controlled; the destiny of the Swazi, or of any small-scale society in the modern world, will in the long run be shaped by external forces, which
can be structurally interpreted.

Economic Growth

There is in modern Swaziland increasing contact with the outside world,
both economically and politically. Economically, Swaziland is booming. The geographical isolation, the safeguard of conservatism, is being rapidly and deliberately broken down. New highways are opening up the territory by connecting
growing urban centers; solid bridges are replacing old ponts and narrow cause-
ways; electricity plants are operating in areas where the candle and oil lamp were
the only known artificial lighting. Trucks, vans, automobiles, buses and taxis
rush past barefoot peasants on the new roads. Small aircraft carry white execu-
tives to and from developing areas in the territory. A contract has been signed for
the building of a railway linking Swaziland with the eastern seaboard at Lou-
renco Marques.

These are tangible signs of a new economic orientation. From being one of the poorer underdeveloped areas, Swaziland is being transformed into an area of promising investment through public loans and private enterprise. The local administration succeeded in raising its first general purpose loan; the British government more than tripled its grants-in-aid; in 1961 the territory received a 2.8 million dollar credit from the World Bank's International Development Association (IDA); private white entrepreneurs, apprehensive of the *apartheid* policy of the Republic of South Africa, transferred capital to Swaziland. A poll tax, paid by Africans and, in Swaziland, also by Europeans, constituted over 40 percent of the total revenue in 1946; it dropped to 5 percent by 1956. Income tax, paid mainly by whites, rose almost correspondingly.

The surface of Swaziland is increasingly being shaped by the use of inanimate power, an index of industrialism. In 1949 the Colonial Development Corporation purchased 105,000 acres in the lowlands for irrigation, agriculture, and ranching, and financed the building of a canal to bring water from the Komati River 40 miles away. Since then two other large and several smaller irrigation schemes have been completed, transforming the agricultural possibilities which had previously been limited to dry-land farming. During the last fifteen years a large-scale forestry industry has developed in the western and northwestern areas of the territory on land previously used for the winter grazing of sheep, which were herded across the South African border. The Colonial Development Corporation, together with the international firm of Cortaulds Ltd. has formed a pulp company with an initial capital of 5 million pounds sterling (approximately 14 million dollars). Two large sugar mills are operating in areas where wild animals once roamed freely; a citrus industry, representing considerable capital investment, is already yielding favorable revenues; rice of good quality is being grown in areas under intensive irrigation.

The enumeration of these innovations does not indicate their sociological effect. Change is not a simple movement "from the traditional to the modern." From the time of Mswati, the social context of the Swazi has included Europeans, and in the colonial situation Europeans and Africans (colonizer and colonized) interacted, borrowing from each other. But activities and benefits have been and are unevenly shared between them. It is the Europeans who, recognizing the rich economic potential of modern Swaziland, have taken the initiative in development. Traditional Swazi leaders did not press for greater ease or speed of communication with the rest of the world. When the idea of a railway was first mooted in the late nineteenth century, the Swazi spokesmen expressed opposition on the grounds that it would lead to an exodus of young people, particularly women, trying to escape family obligations and tribal restraint. The present rulers have accepted the new railway plan as part of a process of modernization, which they are unable to check, but do not necessarily favor. Nor is there any pressure by the Swazi to have highways, railway stations, or landing grounds constructed near key homesteads. The main royal villages are still on dirt roads, which, particularly in rainy weather, are braved by car only by an intrepid driver.

Land for agriculture and pasturage continues to be the foundation of

Swazi existence. By the end of 1959, 51.5 percent of the total territory was available for occupation by the Swazi nation. In addition to the Swazi areas described in Chapter 1, more land was purchased by the Swazi nation, and land known as native land settlement areas was purchased by the government from European owners, or set aside by the government from Crown land. Contact with white systems of land tenure, increasing scarcity of land, and such permanent improvements as fences, wattle plantations, and immovable homes, have led to a greater emphasis on individual rights; but, at the same time, the majority of Swazi still appear to consider that land should be held by the chief as the tribal representative, and that every subject should be entitled to its use in a reciprocal political relationship.

Swazi lack capital and technological training, and many are dubious of the values that are associated with Western investment. Over 90 percent of the irrigated land in the country is owned by whites, who use it for the varied and profitable cultivation of rice, sugar, and citrus fruits. Some 1000 acreas under irrigation were made available at no cost to the Swazi, but by 1961, not many Swazi had taken advantage of the offer. This does not mean that the Swazi are incapable of changing. Largely through the efforts of the Department of Land Utilization (a postwar development) Swazi are adopting more intensive and commercial methods of agriculture. Contour ploughing and other techniques of soil and water conservation are more widely accepted; the purchase of fertilizers has risen, the cultivation of cash crops, especially tobacco and cotton, has increased. Today, there are more self-supporting Swazi farmers than there were ten or twenty years ago. The *Ingwenyama* has appointed a board, known as the Central Rural Development Board, to approve schemes for land use and resettlement plans; this board serves as a counterpart in Swazi area to the Natural Resources Board that operates in freehold farms.

Why, then, have the Swazi not made use of the possibilities opened by irrigation? Is it because of fear on the part of conservatives of appearing too ambitious? Is it because of their suspicion of whites, "who do not usually give something for nothing," or because they prefer their existing mode of agricultural techniques? Research on this and similar situations of resistance to change is required.

The purely economic advantages of individual tenure are weighted against the social and political isolation that it is assumed to predicate. A recent (1960) study by John Hughes revealed that a group of educated Swazi agricultural students foresaw political, economic, and social dangers in individual tenure. Politically, it would entail the loss of effective control that is vested in the traditional rulers: individuals who owned land could "behave like kings" and pay no attention to tribal leaders, nor take part in the annual rituals of tribal unification. Economically, individual ownership could produce a class structure opposed to the traditional hierarchy based on birth, and also give rise to a landless peasantry. Socially, it would undermine the quality of "good neighborliness" that characterizes the Swazi community, which is bound together by the sharing of land. The study stressed the widespread fallacy that "progress" and "traditionalism" must always be opposed and that "progress" inevitably means following a Western model. Individuals who have received Western education may deliberately support certain elements of traditional culture.

Animal husbandry is still a major interest of many conservative Swazi. They own more cattle, goats, sheep, horses, donkeys, pigs, and fowls than the whites, and many Swazi areas suffer from overgrazing. The agricultural and veterinary departments meet considerable resistance to their efforts to improve the land by restricting the number of animals. At the same time, under an order made by the *Ingwenyama* in council, cattle are regularly culled from the herds of Swazi who own more than ten head of cattle. The animals thus acquired are auctioned and a levy on the proceeds is credited to the Lifa or Inheritance Fund, which was started in 1946, both to reduce overstocking and to purchase additional land for the Swazi people.

The economic future of Swaziland is largely dependent on the development of her rich mineral potential, recognized by whites, but not by Swazi, from the early period of contact. There are known deposits of gold, asbestos, barytes, iron, and coal. For many years asbestos was the most profitable investment, contributing some 50 percent of the total value of all exports. With the establishment of a Geological Survey Department in 1945 and a Mineral Development Commission in 1953, there has been a systematic attempt by the administration to stimulate and direct prospecting and further exploitation. Swaziland is being brought increasingly into the network of international finance by exports of mineral wealth to the Republic of South Africa, the United Kingdom, France, Spain, and, most recently, Japan. The domestic economy, in turn, reacts to such world trade conditions as the marketing of lower grade asbestos by Russia and the falling off of demand for andalusite coal by Western Germany. The Swazi people do not own any of the local mines, but are affected by opportunities and conditions of employment. The question of the rights of the Swazi as a nation to mining rental is again under review, reviving the old issue of the interpretation of the concessions granted whites by Mbandzeni.

Despite the economic growth, industrial conditions are still rudimentary. Legal provision for trade unions has existed in the statute books since 1942, and there is also a growing body of deliberate legislation to control the workers' safety, health, and welfare. But the first trade union was formed only in 1962 by workers in the pulp factory, and in the absence of trade unions the administration encourages the appointment of tribal representatives at all major industrial concerns. There is only the beginning of an awareness on the part of the Swazi of the need for workers in mines and factories to develop their own organizations.

Migration

More skilled immigrants are coming into Swaziland; simultaneously, however, unskilled Swazi continue to migrate seasonally and temporarily to more industrialized centers. The total population of Swaziland, enumerated in the census of 1956, was 240,511, of whom 233,214 were Africans, 5,919 Europeans, and 1,378 Eurafricans. The figures included 11,728 Swazi temporarily employed outside the territory and 3,470 "foreign Africans" temporarily employed in Swaziland. Between 1946 and 1956 the African population increased by 51,945, of whom 4,854 were new immigrants. Although non-Swaziland Africans totalled only 8,048, or 3.4 percent of the African population, the number of immigrants had increased by 152 percent. Equally, if not more significant, was the increase in European immigration. Between 1946 and 1956 the European population increased by 84.9 percent compared with an increase of only 16.9 percent in the previous decade. The net natural increase remained fairly constant at between 10 and 15 per 1000, and most of the increase was therefore due to immigration; between the years 1952 and 1959, the European population doubled. But the vast majority of the population, over 90 percent, is still Swazi; it provides the "host" culture, to which the African immigrants adapt, and which the Europeans cannot ignore.

The African immigrants fall into two separate categories. First, there are those who look to Swaziland as a permanent home and seek opportunities denied them in their former place of domicile. They include teachers, progressive farmers, and traders from South Africa, anxious to escape certain restrictions of *apartheid*. Before they can be granted the use of land, symbol of citizenship, they must be accepted by the traditional rulers. Should they want to buy land, they also require the approval of the High Commissioner. In the second category of African immigrants are temporary laborers, brought mainly from Portuguese territory and subject to white employers, not Swazi chiefs. The apparently anomalous situation in which a section of the emerging educated middle class of Africans from the Republic are moving into Swaziland, while roughly 11,000 unskilled and semiskilled Swazi work annually in the Republic and roughly 3,500 Africans from Portuguese territory work in Swaziland, can be explained by political and economic pressures. Crudely stated, political freedom is greater in Swaziland than in either of the other territories, but wages are highest in the Republic, the strongest labor magnet, and lowest in Portuguese territory. For the wage earner, the economic appears to override the political factor. However, it must not be forgotten that each person is motivated by subtler drives than are revealed in gross statistics of migration.

I have not the detailed data to evaluate the political or social effects on tribal life of the continuous process of temporary emigration of large numbers of Swazi males. Conflict in the kinship system, especially in marital relationships, may or may not have become intensified, illegitimacy may or may not have increased, political loyalties may or may not have been weakened. It is difficult, moreover, to isolate migration as a single factor from the total range of intensified pressures to which modern Swazi are subjected. However, it is clear that migrant labor has become an accepted activity; migrants often earn more than they could produce with their present agricultural facilities, and money for tax, food, and clothing has become a necessity of the times. There does not appear to be any marked increase in the number of migrants who abandon their ties with their kin and remain away indefinitely; the majority, irrespective of their employent experiences, retain their Swazi identity and return eventually to their country.

Within Swaziland itself there has developed a greater internal mobility. The highest increase in population (67.7 percent) is in the central district of the midlands, the area that has always allowed for closest settlement and is now the main center of urban development; the lowest increase (14.7 percent) is in the Mankaiana district, the least industrialized. Elsewhere in Africa the new urban and industrialized centers have produced a radical political elite. In Swaziland, with its migrant labor force, centralized political structure, and very recent industrial development, an urban-rural dichotomy is only beginning.

The major concentrations of Swazi people, however, no longer occur in traditional royal homesteads, but in centers of European settlement and development. Approximately 4 percent of the African population resides in recognized urban townships. By 1959, Mbabane, the administrative capital, had an estimated population of 5500 inhabitants, of whom some 4200 were Africans. Bremersdorp, more centrally situated for commerce, had a population of 4300, of whom some 3000 were Africans. The Havelock asbestos mine, the largest local employer of labor, housed over 1000 male Africans. Swazi rulers may still obtain the services of loyal subjects for major state rituals and economic enterprises, such as rebuilding the national shrine hut or moving a royal homestead, but the permanent residents in the capital numbered less than 300.

European immigrants have come mainly from other areas in Africa, particularly the Republic of South Africa and the Portuguese province of Mozambique, where racial tension is threatening economic as well as political stability. It is not possible at this stage to know how many European immigrants will remain in Swaziland, or for how long; they have brought in capital and certain skills and have opened new avenues of local employment. Some have also bought land, which establishes a common interest between them and earlier European settlers, rather than tribal authorities.

Political Developments

The traditional Swazi rulers find their position attacked by new ideologies. A democratic system gives greater recognition to achieved than to ascribed qualifications, and uneducated hereditary local chiefs, in particular, find their authority questioned by more Westernized subjects. New ideas of "freedom" are brought in from outside, and events in other parts of Africa have become topics of conversation in many tribal circles. In the past five years political refugees, white and black, escaping for different periods from the repressive policy and "states of emergency" in the Republic, have moved into Swaziland, and the country is strategically placed in the route of African independence movements.

Swaziland, like Southern Rhodesia and Kenya, is politically complicated by the presence of white settlers. In this respect it is different from Basutoland and Bechuanaland, where whites are restricted to an administrative cadre and to traders and missionaries with limited land rights. The influence of the white-settler controlled Republic of South Africa is strong, and the British government—though it has expressed its opposition to *apartheid* and supports, in principle, the ultimate achievement of African self-government—is sensitive both to the claims of white Swazilanders anxious to preserve their privileges, and to the economic pressures of the white Nationalist government of South Africa.

The colonial administration has, however, struggled increasingly to adjust traditional institutions at both the central and local levels to the demands of a modern government. A great deal of the traditional power structure has been retained. The *Ingwenyama* is recognized as the main Swazi representative, the two councils continue to some extent as before. In addition, a skeleton of the main council sits weekly, or as needed, to transact every-day matters. Close contact with government is maintained through a standing committee, appointed by the *Ingwenyama*-in-council. A new range of functionaries has been brought into existence, and the standing committee consists of a chairman, the treasurer of the Swazi National Treasury, the secretary to the nation, and six representatives from the six administrative districts, who are paid from the Swazi National Treasury. The meetings combine both traditional and modern formalities, and efficiency is not considered their main value. There is still virtually unrestricted discussion and an effort to reach unanimity; if this is not achieved, action is generally delayed for as long as possible.

Swazi legal procedure has been drawn into the more formal structure of the West. Fourteen Swazi courts, two courts of appeal, and a Higher Swazi Court of Appeal were instituted in 1950. Swazi courts are empowered to exercise civil and criminal jurisdiction in most matters in which the parties are Africans. Cases arising from the marriage of Swazi by civil or Christian rites are specifically excluded from their civil jurisdiction, and such cases as witchcraft and murder from their criminal jurisdiction. In other cases Swazi courts administer not only traditional law and custom (subject to certain restraints of Western ethics) but also new rules and regulations issued by recognized Swazi authorities under the Swaziland Native Administration Proclamation and laws authorized by an order of the Resident Commissioner. The personnel, procedure, and powers of Swazi courts are more clearly defined than heretofore, and all judgments are recorded.

The Swazi have been granted additional financial responsibilities through the Swazi National Treasury, which derives revenue from payments by government of proportions of various taxes, all fines and fees from Swazi courts and various other sources. The Swazi treasury now pays the rulers, chiefs, and officers of the Swazi administration and also contributes to agricultural, medical, and educational projects. The institutional separation of administrative, judicial, and financial functions of government is a major innovation, but it must be re-emphasized that these functions themselves were also fulfilled in the traditional system. The present system of parallel administation is expensive and ineffective, as we saw in Chapter 2. Power moves down through a chain of British-appointed officials on the one side and the traditional hierarchy on the other, with conflict centered in a few leading personalities. Educated Swazi, including some of the traditional leaders, recognize the impracticability of the traditional system for reaching rapid and major decisions, but they are seeking to build on certain accepted foundations and do not want an imitation of constitutional techniques developed in alien contexts.

In an attempt to bring Swaziland into line with developments in other British territories, a new constitution is being officially formulated, and the legal expert appointed for this purpose is struggling to reconcile a number of conflicting interests. In the first place, one section of the population, the majority of Europeans, afraid to concede the democratic principle of universal franchise in a society where Africans are an unassailable numerical majority, are striving for racial protection through a qualified franchise. The Swazi themselves are divided in their reaction to the white man's fears of being "swamped" or "suffering retaliation for their previous discrimination." Some Swazi are prepared to accept communal representation as a temporary measure, others reject it outright. The party system is itself criticized by prominent Swazi, including Sobhuza, who argue that the caucus, seen as the essential policy-making instrument, is less "democratic" than the traditional system of tribal councils. Conservative Swazi do not accept the necessity of an organized opposition for political freedom and argue that no "count" should ever be made to expose the extent of disagreement. The retort of the more "modern" Swazi is that dissentients should no longer be treated as traitors.

Swazi, like other Africans, are beginning to experiment with the multiparty system. In 1959, a small group of Africans with white and African supporters outside Swaziland formed the Progressive party, the first "modern" political party in the territory. The local leaders were Dr. Zwane and Mr. Nquku. Dr. Zwane is related to the ritual specialist who accompanied Sobhuza to England in 1926, when the latter appealed, in vain, to the Privy Council on the concession issue.

Dr. Zwane's bonds with the people and with Sobhuza are deep and strong. But he is acutely sensitive to the discrimination imposed by whites on all Africans in the south, and his politics have an African Nationalist motivation and Pan-African affiliation. Mr. Nquku is a Zulu who has lived for many years in Swaziland, where he has held the post of supervisor of schools. As an educated foreigner without recognized ties of kinship or locality to substantiate his claims to loyalty, his position is more difficult and less secure. He lost considerable support in 1961, after having been accused of self-interest and dictatorial behavior. The Progressive party is in process of dividing into splinter parties.

In 1962 a new party, the Swaziland Democratic party, came into existence, with Simon Nxumalo as interim chairman. The Nxumalo family is extremely well known and Nxumalo is the clan name of Sobhuza's own mother and paternal grandmother. The Democratic party appears to be linked indirectly with the nonracial Liberal party in South Africa, but realizes the need to gain support from the traditional rulers of a largely conservative population. The most recent declaration of Democratic party policy decries the use of violence, of any abrupt break with the past, and affirms that it will use only legal and constitutional means to achieve its aims. It asserts its strong opposition to all forms of totalitarianism, such as communism, fascism, and *apartheid,* and its general principles include "the protection of fundamental human rights and the safeguarding of the dignity and worth of the human person irrespective of sex, race, color or creed." Its franchise policy is moderate: "the party" recognizes universal suffrage as the ultimate goal, but opposes its introduction in Swaziland before the people have had an opportunity to acquire more political experience. The party desires the "independence of Swaziland within the Commonwealth to be attained with a minimum of delay required to make Swaziland economically and politically viable." It "favors a constitutional monarchy with the *Igwenyama* as King."

The supporters of new political movements include progressive farmers interested in individual land ownership, and teachers and skilled workmen who resent racially differentiated pay scales and employment opportunities. Though still small in number, this emerging middle class is important because it is in line with the trends toward nationalism that are observable in the rest of Africa. But in Swaziland, the new leaders are aware that the traditional Swazi rulers are still sufficiently strong to be useful allies, and they are reluctant to express open antagonism lest they drive away the mass support required for effective action.

It is clear that while the Swazi are being inducted into the strange language and ideologies of modern political maneuvering, they are still interested in conserving the key symbol of unity—the traditional monarchy—and that existing institutions and loyalties will influence future political alignments for some time. The Swazi appear to be moving towards a specific type of society, a modern nation state, distinct in organization and in goals from the clan, the tribe, and the colony described in Chapter 1, yet retaining a continuity unbroken by revolution. Swaziland is one of the very few territories in Africa in which national aspirations coincide with ethnic and cultural homogeneity, and non-Swazi in the territory are insignificant in number. In Swaziland the spontaneous but indecisive resistance to whites that was characteristic of the earlier periods of contact has grown by fairly gradual stages into a more positive approach, expressed in modern political movements and ideas of "freedom," "democracy," and "self-determination." But experimentation with these new concepts and institutions meets with resistance from entrenched traditionalists, some of whom are Western educated.

As in other areas where whites are a settled and privileged group, Swazi nationalism is influenced by racialism. But the extent of racial tension is itself a variable, and in Swaziland it is not as openly acute as it is in the Republic, nor as it was in Kenya. The explanation of this must be sought in a number of factors, such as the relative distribution of land, economic security, administrative policy, political responsibility, and, by no means least important, in the existing culture and in the personality of the leaders.

In Swaziland national identity is temporarily symbolized by Sobhuza.

Every individual Swazi has a number of other identities, sometimes complementary, sometimes opposed: African as distinct from European and Eurafrican, commoner as distinct from aristocrat, peasant as distinct from proletariat. But African nationalism has not yet become (and may never become) the overriding identity in Swaziland. Although the main cleavage in Swazi society is still between whites and non-whites, the line is not completely rigid. Individual whites have identified with Swazi political, economic, and cultural aspirations. The British government is gradually removing discriminatory practices and a few Westernized Swazi have been brought into a small multiracial circle. The new Swazi elite retain their ties with their more traditional kin and as they come to realize their own potential as Africans, are not prepared to accept patronage or tolerate discrimination. The majority of white settlers, in an effort to retain their privileged position, which they interpret as "security," are beginning to be involved in the political struggle with the more liberal metropole on the one hand, and the democratic locals on the other. Although conservatives complain that they are being "sold down the river by Britain," there are a few Africans who complain that the process of liquidation is not sufficiently fast. It seems that four separate groups are engaged in the struggle for power: first, the traditionalists who are able to use the Swazi National Council as their organization; second, the nonracialist Democratic party, represented by a few educated men of both color groups; third, Swazi nationalists who, through the Progressive party, interact with other African nationalist movements; and finally, white nationalists who support the racialist policy of the Republic of South Africa. There are obviously many crosscurrents in modern Swaziland politics. The machinations of princes in the traditional society appear as pure clique politics with little relationship to any social change, and are on a different political level from the techniques of power politics deployed at the present time.

Social Services

The average Swazi (like the average citizen in other countries) is less immediately concerned with political activities than with more direct personal social services, such as education and health.

There are at present some 300 recognized schools for Africans in Swaziland. The majority of these schools are still controlled by missions, subsidized by government grants-in-aid. The Swazi nation continues to maintain and finance one high school and two primary schools, with a total enrollment of over 700, and some enterprising chiefs or tribal districts encourage nondemoninational tribal schools in more remote areas. The government itself has complete responsibility for nineteen secular schools. Until 1961, all schools were racially segregated. In 1961 one white school admitted non-whites in a process that was not accompanied by any crisis.

Greater interest in education is reflected in the higher proportion of children of both sexes who attend school (approximately 55 percent of school-age children were enrolled in 1959, compared with approximately 30 percent in 1945), an increasing number of pupils in the middle and higher grades, and a growing pride and interest among parents in the children's achievements. Before 1945, little encouragement was given to promising students to strive for university degrees. Now, though the number of students does not warrant a university in Swaziland itself, selected individuals receive government scholarships to attend universities elsewhere. There is a growing recognition among Swazi leaders that the rapid expansion of education, particularly higher and technical education, is essential for the Africanization of the various departments of the administration.

In Chapter 4, I indicated that the traditional rulers were conscious of the danger of cleavage between the educated and uneducated, and between those who identified with Christian missions and those who remained supporters of the tribal priests. The spread of the Separatist churches in the past twenty years has weakened the religious influence of orthodox missions and fostered a recognition of traditional ritual. Moreover, many of the princes and young chiefs, even if they, themselves, have little education, are interested in marrying trained nurses and teachers. These women, recognized as a new elite, belong, or have belonged, to Christian churches. By marrying into the aristocracy, new links are forged between traditional rank by birth and modern status by achievement, and between upholders of the ancestral cult and members of the more universal religion.

Together with educational progress, there has been increased investment in health facilities and services. Three Swazi qualified as doctors in the past ten years, and two of them are practicing in government hospitals in the territory; the third, Dr. Zwane, left the service for private practice and politics. Doctors, hospitals, medical outposts, and various health services are now accepted as part of ordinary living. But again, as in other contact situations, there is a duality in adaptation. The acceptance of new medicines and new medicine men does not automatically eliminate the use of ancient remedies, nor the belief in witchcraft, nor the inspired diagnostician and curer. Though the Western medical service, with its hierarchy of trained personnel, introduced new professional associations and institutions, Western treatment is often an addition to, not a substitute for, the traditional.

Perspective

Modernization increases the range of choice, extends the field of individual development, and also multiplies points of potential conflict. Some localities in Swaziland have become more modernized, or "Westernized," than others through external environmental factors—the site of an industry, irrigation canal, or other technological developments—and/or the responsiveness and initiative of particular chiefs or other influential individuals.

Readiness for change rests in part in discontent with the present and in part in anticipation of future rewards, but there always remains a residuum from the past.

In the trend toward increasing complexity of social interaction, which is characteristic of small-scale societies subjected to Western impact, the residuum may make for stability, or become a focus of increasing conflict. Here a distinction must be drawn between cultural and structural persistence. This chapter has emphasized cultural persistence while indicating that there have arisen simultaneously new political tensions and realignments of interest groups. Structural cleavage between whites and non-whites, between radicals and conservatives, and between landowners and land users has not crystalized as sharply as in other countries where opposition to the entrenched privileges ("stubborn conservatism") of ruling groups has accelerated political revolutions. The position, however, is changing rapidly, and we can anticipate that in Swaziland there will be major clashes, complicated by the presence of white settlers, and the resulting structural changes may radically undermine cultural continuity.

Postscript

Since completing this manuscript in December 1962, there have been several significant developments in Swaziland, including a dramatic strike by Swazi employed by whites in major industries throughout the country. From newspaper reports it appears that the strike was suppressed by arresting the leaders and flying in British troops from Kenya to protect property and persons. There was no bloodshed. The local administration appears to have been unprepared for the crisis and press comments emphasized that the behavior of the Swazi was completely unexpected. I submit that, on the contrary, it was sociologically predictable and that the antagonisms the strike expressed are historically and structurally rooted. The recent constitutional concessions have not produced a balance of power sufficiently different to accord with African developments outside of Swaziland. As could be anticipated from our analysis, Sobhuza as *Ingwenyama* and paramount chief was in an ambivalent position. He could support neither the workers nor the employers and seems to have negotiated with—and even for— both sides. The suppression of this particular strike does not mean an elimination of underlying tensions and to proclaim that Swaziland has "returned to peace" is an unrealistic dream. Similar conflicts can be anticipated unless, or until, there is a radical change in the economic and political alignment of forces.

References Cited

BEEMER, HILDA, 1937, "The Development of the Military Organization in Swaziland," *Africa,* Vol. X, No. 1, pp. 55–74, No. 2, pp. 176–205.
A detailed account of Swazi age groups.
CRONIN, A. M. D., 1941, "The Swazi," *The Bantu Tribes of South Africa,* Vol. VIII, Sec. 4. Cambridge University Press.
A fine photographic record with an introductory article by Hilda Beemer.
GREEN, L. P., and FAIR, T. J. D., 1960, "Preparing for Swaziland's Economic Growth," *Optima,* pp. 194–207.
A clear analysis of recent economic developments with excellent maps.
HUGHES, A. J. R., "Some Swazi Views on Land Tenure, 1962," *Africa,* Vol. XXXII, No. 3, pp. 253–279.
KUPER, HILDA, 1947, *An African Aristocracy.* London: Oxford University Press for the International African Institute.
A full study of the traditional Swazi political system and its economic and religious institutions.
———, 1947, *The Uniform of Color.* Johannesburg: Witwatersrand University Press.
A continuation of *An African Aristocracy,* analyzing the influence of Western civilization on the traditional society.
———, 1952, *The Swazi.* Ethnographic Survey of Africa, Daryll Forde (ed.), London: International African Institute. *Southern Africa,* Part 1, A concise survey of Swazi social conditions, political and economic structure, religious beliefs and practices, technology and art.
MARWICK, B. A., 1940, *The Swazi.* Cambridge: Cambridge University Press. A useful ethnographic monograph.

Recommended Reading

General Reading on the Culture Area

BARNES, JOHN A., 1954, *Politics in a Changing Society.* London: Oxford University Press for the Rhodes-Livingstone Institute.
> An account of the Ngoni, a branch of the Swazi that moved to Northern Rhodesia.

BEATTIE, JOHN, 1960, *Bunyoro, An African Kingdom.* New York: Holt, Rinehart and Winston.
> An excellent case study of a people in east Africa with a political system somewhat similar to that of the Swazi.

BRYANT, A. T., 1929, *Olden Times in Zululand and Natal.* London. Longmans.
> A detailed historical description of the tribes of southeast Africa.

FORTES, M., and EVANS-PRITCHARD (eds.), 1940, *African Political Systems.* London: Oxford University Press.
> Describes the political structure of eight African tribal societies, of which five are Bantu. Of particular relevance is Gluckman's analysis of the Zulu, the Swazi's powerful neighbors to the southeast.

GLUCKMAN, MAX, 1952, *Rituals of Rebellion.* (Frazer Lecture) Manchester: Manchester University Press.
> A stimulating interpretation of rituals, including the Swazi ritual of kingship.

HOLLEMAN, J. F. (ed.), 1962, *Experiment in Swaziland,* Vols. 1, 2. Durban, South Africa: University of Natal, Institute for Social Research.
> An interesting interdisciplinary research experiment producing demographic, economic, and sociological statistics.

HUNTER, MONICA, 1936, *Reaction to Conquest.* London: Oxford University Press for the International Institute of African Languages and Cultures.
> A detailed ethnographic account of the Pondo, an Nguni people with many similarities to the Swazi.

KRIGE, E. J. and T. D., 1943, *The Realm of a Rain Queen.* London: Oxford University Press.

A study of a peaceful Sotho people ruled by a woman whose position is based largely on ritual claims.

MUNGER, EDWIN S., 1962, "Swaziland: The Tribe and the Country," *American Universities Field Staff Reports Service,* Vol. 10, No. 2.

A concise description of some recent economic and political developments.

SCHAPERA, I. (ed.), 1937, *The Bantu-Speaking Tribes of South Africa.* London: Routledge.

A useful ethnological introduction to the main tribal groups of South Africa.

SCHAPERA, I., 1955, *Tswana Law and Custom.* London: Oxford University Press.
A lucid analysis of a tribal system in many respects similar to that of the Swazi.

RADCLIFFE-BROWN, A. R., and FORDE, C. D., 1950, *African Systems of Kinship and Marriage.* London: Oxford University Press for the International African Institute.

A series of essays with a masterly introduction by Radcliffe-Brown, indicating the structure and variety of African kinship systems.

READ, MARGARET, 1959, *Children of their Fathers.* London: Oxford University Press for the International African Institute.

A study of the Ngoni of Nyasaland, who retain many similarities with the Swazi despite separation in space and time.